# BETWEEN THE SEVERN AND THE WYE

A Companion Anthology

*Forest and Vale and High Blue Hill:*
*Poems of Gloucestershire, the Cotswolds and Beyond*

# Between the Severn and the Wye

## Poems of the Border Counties of England and Wales

**Selected by Johnny Coppin**

◆

Wood Engravings by Ray Hedger

THE WINDRUSH PRESS · GLOUCESTERSHIRE

To Gillian with love
and to all our family and friends in the border counties,
and in memory of Alan Hancox

First published in Great Britain by
The Windrush Press
Little Window, High Street
Moreton-in-Marsh
Gloucestershire GL56 0LL

Telephone: 0608 652012
Fax: 0608 652125

British Library Cataloguing in Publication Data
A catalogue record for this book is available from
the British Library

ISBN 0 900075 23 6

Typeset by DP Photosetting, Aylesbury, Bucks
Printed and bound in Great Britain by
Biddles Ltd, Guildford

The illustrations in this book are photographically reproduced from prints proofed from the original boxwood blocks engraved by Ray Hedger.

A limited edition of 75 copies has been hand-printed by Jonathan Stephenson at The Rocket Press directly from each of the full-page engravings. Each print is on Zerkall mould-made paper and is signed and numbered by the artist.

The prints are available at £60 each (inclusive of vat) from The Rocket Press, Blewbury, near Didcot, Oxfordshire (telephone 0235 851046).

# CONTENTS

## THE MOUNTAIN SOURCES · POWYS
(Montgomeryshire and Radnorshire)

## SHROPSHIRE

v

HEREFORDSHIRE

# WORCESTERSHIRE

# GLOUCESTERSHIRE

## GWENT AND SOUTHERN POWYS
(Monmouthshire and Breconshire)

## BRISTOL AND AVON

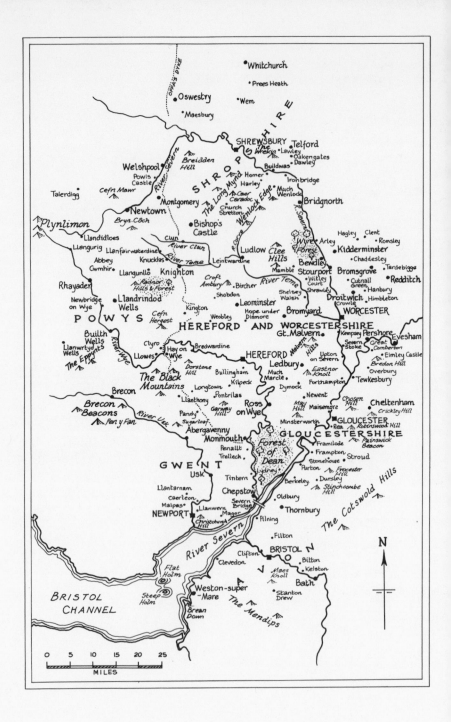

Whitchurch
• Prees Heath
Oswestry
• Wem
• Maesbury

SHROPSHIRE

SHREWSBURY
The Wrekin • Telford
• Lawley • Oakengates
Homer • Dawley
Buildwas

Welshpool
Breidden Hill
Powis Castle
Cefn Mawr
The Long Mynd
Harley
Much Wenlock
Ironbridge

Talerddig
Montgomery
Bryn C8ch
Caer Caradoc
Church Stretton
Wenlock Edge
Bridgnorth

Plynlimon
Newtown
Bishop's Castle

Llandidloes
Clun
River Clun
Ludlow
Clee Hills
Wyre Forest
Arley
Hagley • Clent
• Romsley
Kidderminster
• Chaddesley

Llangurig
Llanfairwaterdine
Knucklas
River Teme
Leintwardine
Mamble
Bewdley
Stourport
Bromsgrove
Tardebigge

Abbey Cwmhir
Llangunllo
Knighton
Croft Ambury
Bircher
Shobdon
River Teme
Witley Court
Shrawley
Shelsey Walsh
Droitwich
Hanbury
Himbleton
Redditch
Cutnall Green

Rhayader
Radnor Hills & Forest
Leominster
Hope under Dinmore
Weobley
Kington
Bromyard
Crowle
WORCESTER

Newbridge on Wye
Llandrindod Wells
Cefn Hergest
POWYS
HEREFORD AND WORCESTERSHIRE
Gt. Malvern
Kempsey
Severn Stoke
Pershore
Great Comberton
Evesham

Builth Wells
Llanwrtyd Wells
The Epynts
Clyro
Hay on Wye
Bredwardine
HEREFORD
Ledbury
Malvern Hills
Upton on Severn
Severn
Elmley Castle
Bredon Hill
Overbury

Llowes
River Wye
Dorstone Hill
Much Marcle
Eastnor Knoll
Forthampton
Tewkesbury

Brecon
The Black Mountains
Longtown
Bullingham
Kilpeck
Dymock
Newent

Brecon Beacons
Pen y Fan
Llanthony
Pontrilas
Garway Hill
Ross on Wye
May Hill
Maisemore
Chosen Hill
Cheltenham
Crickley Hill

River Usk
Pandy
Sugarloaf
Minsterworth
GLOUCESTER
Rea
Robinswood Hill

Abergavenny
Monmouth
Forest of Dean
GLOUCESTERSHIRE
Painswick Beacon

GWENT
USK
Penallt
Trellech
Framilode
Frampton
Stonehouse
Purton
Stroud
Frocester Hill

Llantarnam
Caerleon
Malpas
Tintern
Lydney
Berkeley
Dursley
Stinchcombe Hill
The Cotswold Hills

NEWPORT
Christchurch Hill
Llanwern
Magor
Severn Bridge
Chepstow
Oldbury
Thornbury

Pilning
• Filton

River Severn
Clifton
BRISTOL
• Bitton
• Kelston

Flat Holm
Clevedon
Maes Knoll
Bath

BRISTOL CHANNEL
Steep Holm
Weston-super-Mare
Stanton Drew
The Mendips

Brean Down

N

0   5   10   15   20   25
MILES

X

# INTRODUCTION

'Blessed is the eye between Severn and Wye' so the saying goes, and it is easy to see why many claim the border counties of England and Wales to be the most beautiful in Britain. Here is a landscape that has remained relatively unchanged for centuries. From Plynlimon and the mountains of Mid-Wales where both the Severn, Britain's longest river, and the Wye are born – right down to Chepstow and the Severn estuary where the two rivers finally meet and flow as one.

This is a region of mountains, forests, hills and rivers; a region whose towns and villages, cathedral cities and castles are steeped in history, folklore and romance. This landscape forms the backcloth to the books of Mary Webb, Ellis Peters, and Laurie Lee, and is at the heart of the music of Elgar, Butterworth, Parry and Gurney. It has also continued to inspire generations of poets, artists and craftsmen.

I shall certainly never forget my first impressions of this border country. There was the day I drove to a concert in Shropshire via the three 'L's of Ledbury, Leominster, and Ludlow; the many visits to Hay and the Wye Valley; and how can I ever forget those two rain-soaked days spent walking Offa's Dyke from Kington to Knighton over ten years ago! I certainly never tire of heading for the hills and exploring the back lanes and footpaths of this country, and perhaps it was no coincidence that I married a wonderful 'Shropshire lass' with a passion for the work of Mary Webb.

As a singer and songwriter, I have lived in Gloucestershire for many years, but it was in 1982 that I began to collect poems from the county and set them to music. Many of these were included in my first anthology of poems *Forest and Vale and High Blue Hill*, the album of the same name (launched at the 1983 Cheltenham Festival of Literature), and subsequent albums such as *English Morning*, and *Edge of Day* – a collaboration with and tribute to Laurie Lee. Then in 1988, I was asked by Chris Eldon-Lee of BBC Radio Shropshire to set some Shropshire poems for a live concert broadcast from The Gateway Arts

1

Centre in Shrewsbury. Spurred on by my wife's enthusiasm, I began my research at the Shrewsbury and Madeley libraries, and the result was four songs. These included Mary Webb's 'When the Thorn Blows', and two poems in this anthology – 'The Shropshire Friends' by John Masefield, and Margery Lea's 'On a Hill in Shropshire'. This project marked the beginning of this anthology, as my interest in the border counties was rekindled, and I began to discover more and more poems.

My aim has been to create an anthology of poems that celebrate the 'spirit of place' – poems that particularly evoke the atmosphere and character of the area and its people. This book is very much a personal selection from the hundreds of poems I have collected. In defining the geographical limitations, I have chosen not to adhere literally to the saying '... between the Severn and the Wye', but to venture several miles north and east of the Severn, and west of the Wye – to include all the border counties of England and Wales where the two rivers flow through and spread their influence. This therefore is an area beginning at the source of the rivers at Plynlimon in Powys, broadening out to include Shropshire, Herefordshire, Worcestershire, and Gloucester-shire, and ending with Gwent and Avon where the two rivers meet under the Severn Bridge and flow out to the Bristol Channel. Poems from the Cotswolds have been excluded, except for those set on the edge overlooking the Severn Vale, as many of these can be found in my *Forest and Vale and High Blue Hill* companion anthology. I have omitted poems from Bath as I feel it is a city belonging more to the Cotswolds and old Somerset; and in the Gwent and South Powys section I have restricted myself to Monmouthshire and part of Breconshire – namely, the Usk Valley from Brecon down to Newport.

With regard to the choice of poems, I have not limited myself only to work written by poets born or living in the area, even though naturally enough the greater part of this collection falls into this category. My own personal preference is for twentieth century poetry – that is, poems written in the language of today and that speak most directly; with a few exceptions, this is reflected in my selection. Therefore I have omitted many well-known earlier works found in previous anthologies; by poets such as Shelley, Donne, Pope, Traherne, Vaughan, Churchyard, and Bloomfield; the exceptions are the Hous-man poems, and extracts from Wordsworth, Tennyson, and Kilvert, which all seem to me timeless and still relevant today.

One of the delights in researching this project has been to discover so many excellent poets not known to me before, and most of whom are living in the region. The main problem has been selecting just over a hundred poems from a vast collection because of restrictions imposed by economics and the size of the book. Therefore it has all been a question of striking a balance. There are several poets whose work I would like to have included more of but, limited to just fifteen poems per county, this has not been possible. I have therefore tried to represent a broad range of poets, and at the same time give a balance of places and subjects in each county. Of course there are always a few exceptions as poets are particularly inspired by the spirit of places such as The Black Mountains, the Shropshire hills, Tintern and Kilpeck.

Although I have included some extracts from longer poems, there are many I have had to exclude because they could not be extracted without losing the sense and spirit of the work, and yet were too long to be included in full. Such examples are the Bristol poems of Charles Causley, 'The Littleton Whale' and others by Charles Tomlinson, 'The Usk' by C.H. Sisson, and P.J. Kavanagh's 'Severn Aisling'.

This selection of poems is not all nostalgia for a time and a way of life long passed. By including many poems from both young and current writers, I very much wanted an anthology for today; one that not only celebrates the border counties of England and Wales, but also confronts many of the pressures and issues that affect the region in the 1990s. The book is designed to be read either as a journey 'from the source to the sea', or to be dipped into at random. Some of the poems I have known for a number of years, while most are recent discoveries. I do hope that by reading this book you too will enjoy both the poems and this beautiful border country for many years to come.

Johnny Coppin.
*Gloucestershire,  May 1993.*

# ACKNOWLEDGEMENTS

For kindling my initial enthusiasm and reading through my selection of poems, I sincerely thank my wife Gillian Wall. She has been my guiding star and without her none of this would have been possible.

For helping with my research I'm indebted to and thank the following: the late Alan Hancox, Alan Tucker, Douglas Maclean (and their bookshops in Cheltenham, Stroud and Coleford) plus all the many bookshops in the region; David Hart of West Midlands Arts; Sandra Stevens of the Avon Poetry Foundation; Tim Porter, the Assistant County Librarian, Hereford and Worcestershire; Amy Wack, the Poetry Editor at Seren Books; Alan Halsey of the Poetry Bookshop, Hay-on-Wye; Margaret Austin, Gladys Mary Coles and the Mary Webb Society; Eleanor Cooke; Chris Eldon-Lee and Sue Herbert; Jerry Friar; Lynn Holmes; and David Ashbee of the Holub Poets.

For their co-operation and help I would like to thank the staff at the following libraries: Shrewsbury, Madeley, Bridgnorth, and Telford in Shropshire; Newtown in Powys; Hereford, Worcester, Evesham, Malvern, Ross-on-Wye, Kidderminster, and Stourport in Hereford and Worcestershire; Gloucester, Cheltenham, Stroud, and Cirencester in Gloucestershire; Monmouth and Cwmbran in Gwent; Bristol Central Library and Bath in Avon; and The Poetry Library on the South Bank in London.

For their earlier books and anthologies I am grateful to F. Bradley-Birt, Gordon Dickins, Lawrence W. Hockey, Barry Keogan, David Lockwood and Frederick Grice, Harley Millichap, S.L.I. Pettit, Bill Pickard and Edward Martin, S.F. Gavin Robinson, Guy Stapleton, and Ivor Waters.

A special thank you to all the many poets; firstly, those who have kindly assisted my journey of discovery, and whose work I have been able to select for this anthology; secondly, those who sent in poems in response to my requests, and who suggested other names and avenues to explore; and finally a sincere thank you and apology to those poets whose work I have not been able to include this time.

For capturing the spirit of the border counties in his wonderful wood-engravings, I sincerely thank Ray Hedger and his wife Sally. For keeping the faith and realising this anthology, I especially thank Victoria Huxley and Geoffrey Smith of Windrush Press.

I have had so much encouragement and support from any family and friends and I would like to thank my father Alan, my brothers Richard and his family, Julian and Kate; John, Philomena and Martin Wall; Pamela and Joshua Dempsey; and all my family; Paul and Jane Burgess, Phil Beer and Anna Spacey, Maureen, Freiden and Colette Darwin, Mick Dolan and Glenn Goodman, John and Gill Broomhall, Trevor and Caroline Foster, Gareth Sampson, Mimi Pfeifer, Matt, Bob and Nancy Clifford, Mike, Régine and Lauren Candler, Martin and Jane Fry, Gwen and Roger Dix, Ruth Grocott, David Goodland and Brian Wheeler, Malcolm and Ann Kilminster, Jenny and David Williams, Margaret and Brian Scragg, Karen and Mark Shackleton, John and Cathy Eeles, Al and Jenny Fenn, Geoff and Frankie March, Jerry and Anna Friar, Carolyn Spice and Ken Shaw, John and Aeileish Watts, and so many friends and those on my mailing list.

For their continued support on the airwaves I thank Mike D'Abo, Geraldine McCullagh, Mark Hurrell, Rob Salvidge and Andy Vivien of BBC Radio Gloucestershire; Chris Eldon-Lee, Richard Walker and Mike Naylor of BBC Radio Shropshire; Nonny Dumville of BBC Radio Hereford and Worcestershire; Dave Cartwright of Radio Wyvern; Jon Benns and Chris Mills of BBC Radio South & West; Andy Westgate of GWR Radio; John Turner, Keith Warmington, Roger Bennett, Alli Vowles, and Vicki Klein of BBC Radio Bristol; all at Severn Sound; on national radio – Stuart Hobday and Alan Roberts of BBC Radio 2; on TV – Simon Hammond and Mike Dornan of the BBC; Geoffrey Shepherd, Ken Price, Richard Wyatt and Melitza Palmer of HTV; and Geoff Barratt and Ken Goodwin of Central TV. And for their support in the press I thank John Bilton and David Harrison of the *Bristol Evening Post*; Bev Hawes of the *Western Daily Press*; Tracy Baker and Andy Read of the *Stroud News and Journal*; Allan Guy and Cheryl Jones formerly of the *Stroud Observer*; the staff of the *Gloucester Citizen, Gloucestershire Echo, Wilts. and Glos. Standard, Shropshire Star*, and *Worcester Evening News*; June Lewis and the editor of *Cotswold Life*; John Bright of Forest of Dean Newspapers; Tony Slinger of *Venue* magazine; Pat and Rob Scrase of *Folkwrite*; and *What's On in Shropshire* magazine.

# CREDITS

The publishers would like to credit and thank the following for their kind permission in allowing the use of the poems in this anthology. While every effort has been made to contact the copyright holders, the publishers would be happy to hear from anyone whom they have not been able to trace. Mr Jeffrey Cooper for the extract from 'Ryton Firs' by Lascelles Abercrombie, from *Twelve Idylls*, Martin Secker, 1928. Sam Adams for 'Hill Fort, Caerleon' from *The Boy Inside*, Triskele Press. David Ashbee for 'Elvers' from *Severn Bore Sequence*, 1975. Faber & Faber Ltd for the extract from 'The Malverns' by W.H. Auden, from *On This Island*, 1936, and *The English Auden*, Faber & Faber, 1977. Annemarie Austin for 'Camera Obscura' from *The Weather Coming*, Taxus, 1987. Richard Ball for 'Maesbury' from *Avalon 3*, Outposts, 1969 and 'New Passage Hotel, Pilning' from *Avalon 2*, Outposts, 1969. John Barnie for 'In the Black Mountains' from *Lightning Country*, Dangaroo Press, 1987. John Murray (Publishers) Ltd for 'A Shropshire Lad' and 'Bristol' from *Collected Poems*, 1958. Ruth Bidgood for 'Old Pump-house, Llanwrtyd Wells' from *Given Time*, Christopher Davies Ltd, and *Lighting Candles – New and Selected Poems*, Poetry Wales Press, 1982; and 'Bullingham, Hereford' from *The Point of Miracle*, Gomer Press. Alison Bielski for 'Well at Trellech' from *The Jubilee Anthology of Gwent Poetry Society*, 1981, Mammon Press. D.L. Bowen: 'The Radnor Hills' from *Radnor Hills and Other Poems*, Wilding & Son, Shrewsbury. Carcanet Press Ltd. for 'Apple Country' by Alison Brackenbury, from *Selected Poems*, 1991. Margaret Bramford for 'Pershore' from *The Book of Pershore* by Phillip Barrett, Barracuda, 1980. Geoffrey Bright: 'On Croft Ambury' from *Hereford is Heaven*, Batsford, 1948. Freda Bromhead for 'Stones of Bristol'.Elizabeth Barrett Browning: extract from '*Aurora Leigh*', Chapman & Hall, 1856. Vuyelwa Carlin for 'The Grass Road'. E.B.W. Chappelow: 'The Cabot Memorial Tower' from *West Country Poems*, Channing Press, 1938. The Literary Executor of Leonard Clark for 'At

Clyro' from *The Mirror*, Wingate, 1948; 'Border Country', 'Charcoal Burners', and 'The Forest' from *English Morning*, Hutchinson, 1953; and 'Fathom Five' from *The Way It Was*, Enitharmon, 1980. Carcanet Press Ltd. for 'Sheila na Gig at Kilpeck' by Gillian Clarke, from *Selected Poems*, 1985. Gladys Mary Coles and Duckworth and Co. Ltd for her poem 'Priory Ruins, Much Wenlock' from *Leafburners*, Duckworth, 1986. Doreen Colwill for 'Bridgnorth' by Ronald Colwill from *Lines Fine Drawn*, 1981. Eleanor Cooke for extracts from *Who Killed Prees Heath?* published by Bristol Classical Press and Shropshire Wildlife Trust, 1991. Lewis Glyn Cothi: 'From high Plynlimon . . .' taken from *A Book of the Severn* by A.G. Bradley, Methuen, 1920. W.H. Davies: 'Days that have been' and 'River Severn' from *Collected Poems*, Jonathan Cape, 1942. Roger Davison for 'Barges at Purton' from *Five Particular Places*, Pear Tree Press. John Drinkwater: 'Mamble' from *Swords and Ploughshares*, Sidgwick & Jackson, 1915. Bloodaxe Books for 'Wild Strawberries' by Helen Dunmore, from *The Raw Garden*, 1988. Faber & Faber Ltd for 'Landscapes, III: Usk' by T.S. Eliot, from *Collected Poems 1909-1962*. Margiad Evans: 'The Town II' from *A Candle Ahead*, Chatto & Windus, 1956. U.A. Fanthorpe for 'Purton Lower Bridge' from *Voices Off*, Peterloo Poets, 1984 and 'Stanton Drew' from *Side Effects*, Peterloo Poets, 1978, and both poems in *Selected Poems*, Penguin, 1986. Peter Finch for 'Severn Estuary ABC' from *Selected Poems*, Seren, 1987. Catherine Fisher for 'Severn Bore' from *Immrama*, Seren, 1988. Oxford University Press Ltd for 'Passing Newbridge-on-Wye' by Roy Fisher, from *Poems 1955-1987*, OUP, 1988. Rose Flint for 'Cariad' from *Blue Horse of Morning*, Seren, 1991. Carcanet Press Ltd for 'Buzzard Soaring' by Roger Garfitt, from *Given Ground*, 1989. Gwen Grice and David Lockwood for 'Cathedral City' by Frederick Grice, from *Blue Remembered Hills* anthology, 1980. Paul Groves for 'The Forest of Dean'. Penny Ely, Trustee of the Ivor Gurney Estate for 'Song', 'Tewkesbury', and extract from 'The Old City – Gloucester' from *Collected Poems*, OUP, 1982; and 'The Lock-keeper' from *War's Embers*, Sidgwick & Jackson, 1919. Alan Halsey for 'A Short Guide to the Carvings at Kilpeck' from *The Kilpeck Anthology*, ed. Glen Storhaug, Five Seasons Press, 1981. Patrick Harvey for 'On Painswick Beacon' by F.W. Harvey, from *September and Other Poems*, Sidgwick & Jackson, 1925. Michael Henry for 'Dursley Lantern'. Paul Henry for 'Penallt, 1981' from *Time Pieces*, Seren, 1991. André Deutsch Ltd for extract from 'Mercian Hymns' by Geoffrey Hill, from *Collected Poems*, 1986. Carcanet Press Ltd for 'Worcestershire Lanes' by Molly Holden, from *Selected Poems*, 1987; 'Floods at Bewdley' from *Air and Chill Earth*, Chatto & Windus, 1971. Jeremy Hooker for 'Tintern Abbey: the white wind', from *Guests of Silence*. Gavin Hooson for 'On Cefn Mawr' – first appeared in the *Anglo-Welsh Review*. Rex F. Hopes: 'Clevedon' from *The Ship and Castle*, Henry Hill Ltd, 1939. Bloodaxe Books Ltd for 'Old Song' by Frances Horovitz, from *Collected Poems*, 1985. A.E. Housman: 'The Welsh Marches' and 'Bredon Hill' from *A Shropshire Lad*, Kegan & Paul, 1896; 'The First of May' from *Last Poems*, Grant Richards, 1922. Donald Hughes: extract from 'The Wye' from *Songs from the Ship & Castle*, Bristol, 1934. Jo Hunt: 'Worcestershire Lad' and extract from 'Severn' from *Worcestershire Lad*, Market Place Press, 1977. Robin Ivy for 'Severn' from *Worcestershire Suite*, 1992. Ivan Jones for 'Ironbridge' from *Borderlines V*, 1987. T. Harri Jones: 'Abbey Cwmhir' from *Collected Poems*, J.D. Lewis, 1977. Castlebury Books for 'Note on History' by Edward Kaulfuss, from *Roses at Midnight*. Francis Kilvert: extract from 'Hill Flowers', from *Collected Verses*, Kilvert Society, 1968. Margery Lea for 'At Powis Castle, Montgomeryshire' and 'On a Hill in Shropshire' from *These Days*, Wilding & Son, Shrewsbury, 1975. Peters, Fraser & Dunlop Group Ltd for 'On Beacon Hill' by Laurie Lee, from *Selected Poems*, André Deutsch, 1983. Katrina Burnett for 'The Birthright' by Eiluned Lewis, from *Morning Songs and Other Poems*, Macmillan, 1944. Hilary Llewellyn-Williams for 'The Bee-Flight' from *Book of Shadows*, Seren, 1990. Robin Lloyd: 'Bristol Fashion' from *600 years of Bristol Poetry*, ed. Edward Martin and Bill Pickard, Bristol, 1973. Tessa Lund for 'The Black Mountains' from *A Grass Blade Between Thumbs*, Enitharmon, 1988. The Society of Authors as the Literary Representative of the Estate of John Masefield for the extract from *Wonderings*, Heinemann, 1943; 'On Eastnor Knoll' from *Collected Poems*, Heinemann, 1923; 'The Shropshire Friends' from *In Glad Thanksgiving*, Heinemann, 1966. Geoffrey Mason for 'Carpenters (Much Marcle)'. Roland Mathias and Gomer Press for 'Departure in Middle Age', from *Burning Brambles*, Gomer, 1983. Christopher Meredith and Seren Books for 'Another Go at Hay Bridge', from *Snaring Heaven*, Seren, 1990. Len Mullan for 'Landscape'. Poetry Wales Press Ltd for 'At Usk' by Leslie Norris, from *Selected Poems*, 1986. Sybil Powis: 'Goodbye to the Hills' from *Upland and Valley*, Wilding & Son, 1941. Peter Reading for 'Mortimer Forest' from *The Municipality's Elderly*, Secker & Warburg, 1974. Arthur L. Salmon: extract from 'In the Dim City' from *West Country Verses*, Blackwood, 1908. Dave Sampson: 'Bristol, An Exile's

View' from *Bristol Evening Post*, and *600 Years of Bristol Poetry*, ed. Edward Martin and Bill Pickard, Bristol, 1973. Sheila Simmons for 'Stroudwater Shades'. Carcanet Press Ltd and C.H. Sisson for 'Eastville Park' from *Anchises*, 1976, and *Collected Poems*, 1984. Oxford University Press Ltd for the extract from 'Green Mountain, Black Mountain' by Anne Stevenson, from *Minute by Glass Minute*, OUP, 1982. Guida Swan: 'Bristol Re-visited' from *Bristol Re-visited and Other Poems*, Cock Robin Press, 1977. Alfred Lord Tennyson: extract from 'In Memoriam A.H.H.' from *The Complete Poetical Works of Tennyson*, OUP, 1953. Edward Thomas: 'The Mountain Chapel' from *Collected Poems*, Selwyn & Blount, 1920. G. Thomas for 'The Lonely Farmer' by R.S. Thomas, from *An Acre of Land*, Montgomery, 1952. John Tompkins: 'Clifton Suspension Bridge' from *Portraits of Bristol*, Kingsmead, 1977. Oxford University Press Ltd for 'At St Mary's Church' by Charles Tomlinson, from *The Way In and Other Poems*, 1974, and *Collected Poems*, 1985. Tricia Torrington for the extracts (parts 2 and 3) from 'Train'. Gael Turnbull: 'At Witley Court' from *Finger Cymbals*, Satis, 1971; 'A Hill' from *A Trampoline*, Cape Goliard, 1968. Robert Wade: 'The Wye at Hereford' from *Verses*, Orpheus Press, Leominster. Brian Waters: extract from *The Bristol Channel*, Dent, 1955. Ivor Waters: 'Foresters' and 'Chepstow' from *Poems*, Moss Rose Press, 1987. Mary Webb: 'The Mountain Tree' and 'Hill Pastures' from *Fifty-one Poems*, Jonathan Cape, 1946. Eric Walter White: 'Brean Down' from *The Room and Other Poems 1921–26*, High House, 1927. Jonathan Williams: extract from 'Serenade', from *The Loco Logodaedalist in Situ*, Cape Goliard, 1971 and *The Kilpeck Anthology*, Five Seasons, 1981. Merryn Williams for 'Hang-gliders' © Merryn Williams. William Wordsworth: extract from 'Lines Written a Few Miles Above Tintern Abbey' from *Wordsworth, Poetical Works*, OUP, 1904. The Andrew Young Estate for 'At Arley' by Andrew Young, from *Complete Poems*, Secker & Warburg. David Higham Associates Ltd for the extracts from 'Songs of the Three Rivers' by Francis Brett Young, from *The Island*, Heinemann, 1944; extract from 'Testament' from *Poems 1916–18*, Collins, 1919.

# THE MOUNTAIN SOURCES
## POWYS
(Montgomeryshire & Radnorshire)

From high Plynlimon's shaggy side
Three streams in three directions glide;
To thousands at their mouth who tarry,
Honey, gold, and mead they carry.
Flow also from Plynlimon high
Three streams of generosity;
The first a noble stream indeed
Like rills of Mona runs with mead;
The second bears from vineyards thick
Wine to the feeble and the sick;
The third till time shall be no more
Mingled with gold shall silver pour.

LEWIS GLYN COTHI (*trans.*)

# from *Songs of the Three Rivers*

(from *The Island*)

Severn is born of the sodden mosses
Where smooth Plynlimon's dome is bowed
Under the rain the West Wind tosses
From tattered fleeces of sea-born cloud;
Where the sour-grass moors lie wet and wan,
And the mawn-pool's mirror is misted grass,
And the skirts of the sky's pavilion
Daggle the lint-white cotton grass;
Where wild the curlew whinnies and cries
And whimbrels wheel in windy weather
And buzzards peck at the glazing eyes
Of sick lambs lost in the rain-lodged heather.
Only the carrion wings rejoice
Screaming above the smell of slaughter;
For the mountain's voice is but the voice
Of wind-stripped grasses and welling water . . .

FRANCIS BRETT YOUNG

# The Lonely Farmer

Poor hill farmer astray in the grass:
There came a movement and he looked up, but
All that he saw was the wind pass.
There was a sound of voices in the air,
But where, where? It was only the glib stream talking
Softly to itself. And once when he was walking
Along a lane in spring he was deceived
By a shrill whistle coming through the leaves:
Wait a minute, wait a minute – four swift notes;
He turned, and it was nothing, only a thrush
In the thorn bushes easing its throat.
He swore at himself for paying heed,
The poor hill farmer, so often again
Stopping, staring, listening, in vain,
His ear betrayed by the heart's need.

R.S. Thomas

# Cariad

(Set on the A470 near Talerdigg)

Between hills plump as hens the summer road
speeds cars, bisects the bee-danced hedges;
a man, there, on the dangerous edge,
flaps and stutters, slurred feet swerving
in and out the verge, the blurred flowers.

His chin has fallen away from his stained face
with the weight of the whisky.
He is all weight, a big man in his bones,
dead heavy to have on our hands:
*Where do you live?* we ask him.
*Over the hill, cariad,*
*over this little Welsh hill.*

Inches away, isolate people
flash past us fast as a film
reeling the road up from the beaches.
He rocks to and fro, calls me *cariad,*
enters our car with confusion:
*But you're English . . .*

His farm lies in a sty of nettles.
In the bird echoes linger voices:
wife and daughter
tragedy ghosting quietly over the gate.
*What is the answer, cariad?*
Blue eyes washed by his own long rain
stare down the valley; the cuckoo trees,
the sepia river. *The finest fishing*
*you'd be welcome . . .*

The geography of his ruined heart
puzzles the wavering, changing boundaries,
the mirages of gentle friendly hills.

ROSE FLINT

# The Mountain Chapel

Chapel and gravestones, old and few,
Are shrouded by a mountain fold
From sound and view
Of life. The loss of the brook's voice
Falls like a shadow. All they hear is
The eternal noise
Of wind whistling in grass more shrill
Than aught as human as a sword,
And saying still:
' 'Tis but a moment since man's birth
And in another moment more
Man lies in earth
For ever; but I am the same
Now, and shall be, even as I was
Before he came;
Till there is nothing I shall be.'
Yet there the sun shines after noon
So cheerfully
The place almost seems peopled, nor
Lacks cottage chimney, cottage hearth:
It is not more
In size than is a cottage, less
Than any other empty home
In homeliness.
It has a garden of wild flowers
And finest grass and gravestones warm
In sunshine hours
The year through. Men behind the glass
Stand once a week, singing, and drown
The whistling grass
Their ponies munch. And yet somewhere,
Near or far off, there's a man could
Live happy here,
Or one of the gods perhaps, were they
Not of inhuman stature dire,
As poets say
Who have not seen them clearly, if

At sound of any wind of the world
In grass-blades stiff
They would not startle and shudder cold
Under the sun. When gods were young
This wind was old.

EDWARD THOMAS

The Mountain Chapel

# The Mountain Tree

Montgomery's hills are deeply brown,
In Merioneth the sun goes down,
And all along the Land of Lleyn
The spate of night flows darkly in.

Come away to the mountain tree!
Cinnabar-red with fruit is she.
We'll watch the stars, like silver bees,
Fly to their hive beyond the seas.

MARY WEBB

# On Cefn Mawr

The moon drew me out from behind the glass
Mud-weary from a week of rain
To the ridge's high back, looking North.

After seven days in the belly of a cloud
The moon it was that gave me distances –
A hard rim against the darkening sky,
The one stark tree as brittle as frost.
Here autumn wore the white owl's face.
The hips and haws that kindle the hedgerow
Were daylight's gauds cast off. All colour
Drained down to the valley's sump.
Night had taken back her homeland
Where farm and chapel were now her daydreams.

A cow shifted her bulk by the hedgerow,
Muffled in her own steam. Like me
She was stranded by the light's neap tide.

In the silence then that fixed the stars
I turned my alien footsteps homeward.

Before morning
In the dark vault of my sleeping skull
The Pole Star spun the black dome.

GAVIN HOOSON

# At Powis Castle, Montgomeryshire

Gaunt bulwark, grown out of rock and stone,
A slow agglomerate of history;
Girt by forest and chronicled in rune.
Bulking black in a dawn light it stands,
Time-recording, indigenous as a tree,
Sentinel over the far, stern sunless lands
From which it grew.
                        Its statues, balustrade,
The dark severity of square-clipped yew,
And fir and pine, giant sombre courtiers, ring
Its formal grandeur. Housing duke and king,
It has known pride, ambition, strife and greed.

And there, in a room of gilded splendour, massed
With ornament and solemn tapestry,
A human foot has left – all else decayed –
This small pathetic memory of the past:
A woman's shoe, embedded in masonry
Three hundred years ago. Perhaps she searched
In vain; confessed its loss to nurse or maid;
Limped, laughing, round the ornate bed, or watched
Barefooted for a lover at the high window.
Twenty-five frail bones that slipper encased –
And all are dust; the dust of an earl's daughter.
And the staunch walls repel no marauders now,
Echoing only tourists' voices and laughter.

MARGERY LEA

# The Birthright

We who were born
In country places,
Far from cities
And shifting faces,
We have a birthright
No man can sell,
And a secret joy
No man can tell.

For we are kindred
To lordly things,
The wild duck's flight
And the white owl's wings;
To pike and salmon,
To bull and horse,
The curlew's cry
And the smell of gorse.

Pride of trees,
Swiftness of streams,
Magic of frost
Have shaped our dreams:
No baser vision
Their spirit fills
Who walk by right
On the naked hills.

EILUNED LEWIS

# Abbey Cwmhir

Cowpasture and the ragged line
Of a ruined wall. A few more cartloads
Of dressed stone filched for a new farmhouse
Or sections of clustered column taken for a cheesepress
And there would be nothing, less even
Than these scrappy remains under the big trees.
The coffin-lid of an old abbot is propped up
Behind the door of the Victorian church,
That's all. Heavy with July the elms
Remember nothing.

        Appropriately
There is no signpost, not even a fieldpath
To the place where they brought the hacked trunk,
Who were they, I wonder, who lugged him here,
All that was left of him, after the English
Had done their thing, what went on in their minds,
Conventional piety, simple human pity
Or the cosmic grief the Son of the Red Judge
Sang into the stormwind, as they urged the pony
Felted with its winter coat, and over the crupper
The bloody carcase, along the bad ways?

Centuries later, in high summer, I feel the cold.

T. HARRI JONES

# Passing Newbridge-on-Wye

All the space under the bridge
fills with the light
of the bare ash-trees and the stone:

what glitter the softness has
comes from the February sun
striking across the pebbles of the riverbed;
there's nothing else.

   The pale light bursts
the distance of the valley as if
in a water-drop on a windscreen,
but in a fullness
with no sharp instant of design:
it's not for catching.

                    The turn
towards the south at the bridgehead
dissolves to a state of the air,

a state the road rests into
as it passes over.

So you can be clouded
with clarities in the act
of crossing the undemanding water.

ROY FISHER

# The Radnor Hills

The untrodden hills of Radnor
Are of my youth a part
Though I never more may see them
I hold them in my heart.

The dark steeps of the Forest
With Whimble as her crown,
The tawny heights of Bryn Côch
Where the Teme springs clear and brown,
The lofty, wind-swept buttress
That Crûg Eryr keeps,
And the castle hill of Knucklas
Where the brook called Ffrwdwyn leaps.

Sheep feed on uplands scented
With drifts of sweet woodruff
With chrome and purple pansies
And golden 'shoes', enough
To furnish all the gypsy horde
To tread the stair-case of the Lord.

O to climb up from Llangunllo
To lone St. Michael's Pool,
To hear the curlew calling
When the evening dusk is falling
And the air is still and cool!

D.L. BOWEN

The Radnor Hills

# Old Pump-house, Llanwrtyd Wells

The door is open. I shall not be intruding,
going in to sit on the bench by the wall,
to breathe the stuffy dankness streaked with sulphur,
and stare through broken panes over the shaggy grounds.
This sociable place has died through lack of visiting.
A pungent drip, still slowly forced from the spring's heart,
has grown a fungus-garden in the great mirrored basin.
Some chairs lie on the sheep-fouled floor,
some lurch, still conversationally grouped,
against the counter over which was handed
health by the tumblerful when crowds came here,
laughing and garrulous, to take the waters;
pulling faces over the taste of their cure,
and bragging of the glasses they had drunk
like boys about their beer. They came streaming
six times a day from the bursting village
to jostle and gossip round the sulphur-bar.
Sheep-farmers, knitting wives, holiday miners
from the black valleys, jam-packed the houses,
ate meals in shifts, and sat outside singing hymns
on the suddenly hushed street of evening;
or went back in warm dusk to the well-house
to hear the Builth harper play under summer trees
and watch the youngsters dance.
The plucked notes, never wholly gay, and laughing voices
spiralled up through the trees, up the long valley;
and lost themselves among the hills
over the sealed frontier of the past.

RUTH BIDGOOD

# from *Hill Flowers*

It fell upon an April day,
When April showers were falling,
And from Dolsylyn, misty grey,
The cuckoo's voice was calling;
Beside the rippling winds of Wye,
So softly, swiftly, flowing,
From fair Wyecliff to Llowes I
At eventide was going.

And when I reached the Otter's Pool,
The golden spires were sighing,
The hills wrapped in rain, and cool
A white storm skudded flying;
Adown Cilceni's dingle side
The mountain rain was pouring,
Past Ty-ly-byngam deep and wide
The mountain brook was roaring . . .

FRANCIS KILVERT

# At Clyro

The foxgloves light the tangled fern,
The honeysuckle trails its way,
And in the fields the mowers turn
And rake in heaps the smoking hay.

The silent pools reflect the sky,
The dams are tight with choking weed,
Thin mists upon the river lie
And undisturbed the young trout feed.

The turf is soft upon the fells,
The sheep stream out from fold and pen,
The Clyro ringers fire their bells
And Kilvert walks his hills again.

LEONARD CLARK

# Another Go at Hay Bridge

Each week at seven I've come back
to this bridge, each time remarked
how the tilting earth shaves away daylight.

There was blue, and the swept bank piled
with trees. Marking flow, weed ropes were
intricate with leaves on the pebbled bed

and sprays of cloud came west another time
ruddled, orange, and the pit above
indigo and around me amethyst.

In the corridor of turned trees
I've stood with my head in the skydome
by constant discs of mars and jupiter

and after, the milky way a semen river
washing cygnus and auriga
arched over me.

Now black trees hunch. Beneath in clamming mist
the river's slicked with clouded mercury,
the weeds gashed dark,

                    as the earth
tilting, pares its minute from the day
and lamps smirch orange globes on air.

I shrink into my coat, turn back.
There'll be frost soon but, too, the pleiades.
Somewhere above the other river runs.

CHRISTOPHER MEREDITH

# SHROPSHIRE

*... Severn flows*
*With the graveness of a deepening stream,*
*Till her waters part – and high in air*
*The steeple vanes of Shrewsbury dream*
*Caught within her silver snare,*
*And her voice is stilled; for now she hath*
*Forgotten the madrigals that she sung*
*In the dalliance of her downward path*
*And the lilt of the valleys where she was young ...*

Francis Brett Young
from *Songs of the Three Rivers*
(from *The Island*)

# On a Hill in Shropshire

There is a ring of beeches on the hill
Lifting to the quiet evening sky
Layered tracery of green and grey,
Voicing reed-like in the hill-wind's sigh
Tales of long ago and far away.
Beneath them lies the valley wide and still.

There is forgetfulness within this ring,
Where memory's steeped in calm and thought is stilled.
For they the secrets of old earth enfold
Within their shadowed forms whose crowns are filled
With lustre of the west and evening gold,
And in the listening silence seem to sing.

MARGERY LEA


# from *Mercian Hymns*

Cohorts of charabancs fanfared Offa's province and
his concern, negotiating the by-ways from Teme
to Trent. Their windshields dripped butterflies.
Stranded on hilltops they signalled with plumes
of steam. Twilight menaced the land. The young
women wept and surrendered.

Still, everyone was cheerful, heedless in such days:
at summer weekends dipping into valleys beyond
Mercia's dyke. Tea was enjoyed, by lakesides where
all might fancy carillons of real Camelot vibrating
through the silent water.

Gradually, during the years, deciduous velvet peeled
from evergreen albums and during the years more
treasures were mislaid: the harp-shaped brooches,
the nuggets of fool's gold.

GEOFFREY HILL

33

# Hill Pastures

High on the hill the curlews and the whimbrels,
Go mating all day long with a sweet whistle;
With a sound of chiming bells and shaken timbrels,
And silver rings that fall in a crystal cup.
They laugh, as lovers laugh when the moon is up,
Over the cotton-grass and the carline thistle.

Poised in his airy spiral the snipe is calling,
Summoning love with a music mournful and lonely
As a lost lamb in the night, rising, falling,
Stranger than any melody, wilder than song.
He cries of life that is short, and death that is long,
Telling his dusky love to one heart only.

Once in seven days a plaintive ringing
Sounds from the little chapel high in the heather,
Out with the sorrowful snipe and the whimbrel winging.
The wild hill ponies hear it there as they graze,
And whinny, and call to their foals, and stand at gaze,
Hearing a clear voice in the clear weather.

And out of pine-dark farms and windy places,
And quiet cottages low in the valley hiding,
Brown folk come with still and wistful faces.
Straying by twos and threes, like the peaceful sheep,
Into the small brown shippen of souls they creep,
Seeking a calm like the hills', but more abiding.

MARY WEBB

34

Hill Pastures

# The Grass Road

The grass road, smooth and wide
through many fields, has a
landscaped look: cattle speck

its vista, motionless, paint-
fresh piebalds:
the far bull
is an ivory idol. – Statued

sward, long green accord,
it is like old palace-
gardens – those that lay peaceful

in late slants of sun,
before the clogs
came claying,
smashing the laughing stones
of the splendid ladies and lords.

VUYELWA CARLIN

# Maesbury

I, who go back to my world,
see from the tall hill, all lie,
and always, like staves,
the sutured face of my country
bears no veins of new green,
but only stone of young, strange settlers.

I, who go back to my land,
live in a lean change,
rasped by eternal weathers,
that pare away some features,
yet do I pour an eye,
into distance grandly
across a mirage of time,
time that would cage my words,
words that mould my stares.

Now, in these loose moments,
not of the spinning tracks of sound,
or a new, tarred geography,
I stand, tied to this place by peace,
in the short days of the showering suns;
O let these words tell of my joy
to worlds, that I am here,
now, and always.

Village of first loves, and laughter,
crush me with the fingers of your Spring,
trace down all my days
the tresses of your living green,
and spin the warm trades
with a delight that lights all ways,
and shakes the wheel of seasons
in the beaks of flame.

Marl, and heft of stone,
scour of oceans, sprawl of reef, and cliff
hurl shadows, and strange tongues of light
to the mind, wondering about histories.
Starry young glances
see only grass, and leaves,
but mine, old as death,
catch with the violet eye, old stances,
some new griefs, and,
in the anchoring clay,
an impeaching stain of Siluria.

RICHARD BALL

# from *Who Killed Prees Heath?*

*I. Voices*

A beat missed, a forgotten score,
marked with sudden bursts of hangars.
Buildings, patched with squares of sky,
squat under roofs of corrugated
moss. A century of tramps
tread green roads to warm byngs:
without so much as a curious glance
behind, workhouse droppings from Wem
and Whitchurch lead armies of concrete
trench and crater, plant runways,
and scuff the common sod to crumbling
shelters that stumble like midday
moles down broken steps. . . .


*VI. Still I cried, Waken, Master,*
*for now is the hour and time.*

Smoke rises from the sweep of bracken,
where the Fox Field limps past forgotten
Sundays. The smell of wood burning,
dry elder practising alchemy in the rain.

A glimpse of red, red roof of caravan
startles a grey sky: the warm smell
of earth, of words melting like summer
snow. The ground moves on an unseen axis.
Ghosts tread an imagined path, move

on, on the road, the last – is it? –
stopping place, on the last common
the last word – *He saw by the rose*
*and the mantle so green that his love had been there*
*and was gone.* . . .

ELEANOR COOKE

39

The English Bridge, Shrewsbury

# The Welsh Marches

(from *A Shropshire Lad*)

High the vanes of Shrewsbury gleam
Islanded in Severn stream;
The bridges from the steepled crest
Cross the water east and west.

The flag of morn in conqueror's state
Enters at the English gate:
The vanquished eve, as night prevails,
Bleeds upon the road to Wales.

Ages since the vanquished bled
Round my mother's marriage-bed;
There the ravens feasted far
About the open house of war:

When Severn down to Buildwas ran
Coloured with the death of man,
Couched upon her brother's grave
The Saxon got me on the slave.

The sound of fight is silent long
That began the ancient wrong;
Long the voice of tears is still
That wept of old the endless ill.

In my heart it has not died,
The war that sleeps on Severn side;
They cease not fighting, east and west,
On the marches of my breast.

Here the truceless armies yet
Trample, rolled in blood and sweat;
They kill and kill and never die;
And I think that each is I.

41

None will part us, none undo
The knot that makes one flesh of two,
Sick with hatred, sick with pain,
Strangling – When shall we be slain?

When shall I be dead and rid
Of the wrong my father did?
How long, how long, till spade and hearse
Put to sleep my mother's curse?

A.E. HOUSMAN

# The Shropshire Friends

Long since, when coming from the West,
With England near, I could not rest,
Though night time fell,
So near the two that I loved best.

There, somewhere, nor-nor-east from me,
Was Shropshire, where I longed to be,
Ercall and Mynd,
Severn and Wrekin, you and me.

So up I went, to walk the deck,
To gaze, with eager aching neck,
For England's Lights,
The Lighthouses preventing wrecks.

Far forward I would crane, to spy
Those fixed stars of the sailor's eye,
His most loved stars,
And feel their beauty drawing nigh.

There, while the beating engines shed
The mumble of their trampled tread,
The ship's great heart,
I stared into the night ahead.

Into a darkness now I stare
Towards where Wrekin lifts in air
And Severn glides,
I know that you are somewhere there.

JOHN MASEFIELD

# Landscape

I drive with the sun at my back
the car's shadow shifting
with each bend and curve
the road, dandelion-fringed,
dropping between Homer and Harley
to climb through birch and oak
to skirt the Edge
higher than cooling tower, abbey and farm.

Beneath the brooding Wrekin
the Severn ambles and turns
easing itself through wood and gorge.
No quickening of spirit
discernible in the steady flow,
it cuts through country once nurtured
to repel and sustain,
past settlements cushioned by hills and fields,
permanent and unquestioning
evolved to the earth's pattern
fashioned in stone cleaved
from where the same hands
ploughed and scythed
flailed and threshed.

LEN MULLAN

# Priory Ruins, Much Wenlock

pale roses cloistered
where white robed doves
inhabit high corridors

petal fragments fallen
in the transept
like lost psalms

my soul responds, dilates
seeing you there
in the green nave
holding a white rose
pure as Shropshire air

GLADYS MARY COLES

# Ironbridge

That short span of iron rests, like man,
On slopes that slip into the abyss:
A paltry edifice to progress
Forced out of sulphured lung and suffering.

Let us forge Museums of gloss,
Applaud the avarice, still repeated;
Burn human dross, forget their loss,
Bleach black bones in the acids of the fêted.

As Severn drifts beneath endlessly,
Heavy with blood and the stench of industry,
That small arch is raised against the sky,
A spider's web – in which the trapped men lie.

IVAN JONES

Ironbridge

# A Shropshire Lad

*N.B. – This should be recited with a Midland accent.*
Captain Webb, the swimmer and a relation of Mary Webb by
marriage, was born at Dawley in an industrial district in Salop.

The gas was on in the Institute,
    The flare was up in the gym,
A man was running a mineral line,
    A lass was singing a hymn,
When Captain Webb the Dawley man,
    Captain Webb from Dawley,
Came swimming along the old canal
    That carried the bricks to Lawley.
        Swimming along –
        Swimming along –
        Swimming along from Severn,
And paying a call at Dawley Bank while swimming along to Heaven.

The sun shone low on the railway line
    And over the bricks and stacks,
And in at the upstairs windows
    Of the Dawley houses' backs,
When we saw the ghost of Captain Webb,
    Webb in a water sheeting,
Come dripping along in a bathing dress
    To the Saturday evening meeting.
        Dripping along –
        Dripping along –
        To the Congregational Hall;
Dripping and still he rose over the sill and faded away in a wall.

There wasn't a man in Oakengates
    That hadn't got hold of the tale,
And over the valley in Ironbridge,
    And round by Coalbrookdale,
How Captain Webb the Dawley man,
    Captain Webb from Dawley,
Rose rigid and dead from the old canal
    That carries the bricks to Lawley.
        Rigid and dead –
        Rigid and dead –
        To the Saturday congregation,
Paying a call at Dawley Bank on his way to his destination.

JOHN BETJEMAN

## *Bridgnorth*

Great sandstone rock, steep fashioned for defence
    That Norman castle Cromwell overwhelmed
Fortress and prison, royal residence
    Whose walks King Charles dubbed finest in his realm.
It is the finest star on Severnside
    Glowing with old half-timbered urbane lustre
An upstairs-downstairs town that may provide
    Two levels for a friendly filibuster.
Poised on their rock High-Towners condescend
    To scan the lesser mortals down below
While in the depths Low-Towners do pretend
    Bridgnorth expires when over Bridge you go.
Perhaps the valley has the final word
In Low Town cemetery all are interred.

RONALD COLWILL

# The First of May

The orchards half the way
From home to Ludlow fair
Flowered on the first of May
In Mays when I was there;
And seen from stile or turning
The plume of smoke would show,
Where fires were burning
That went out long ago.

The plum broke forth in green,
The pear stood high and snowed,
My friends and I between
Would take the Ludlow road;
Dressed to the nines and drinking
And light in heart and limb,
And each chap thinking
The fair was held for him.

Between the trees in flower
New friends at fairtime tread
The way wherè Ludlow tower
Stands planted on the dead.
Our thoughts, a long while after,
They think, our words they say;
Theirs now the laughter,
The fair, the first of May.

Ay, yonder lads are yet
The fools that we were then;
For oh, the sons we get
Are still the sons of men.
The sumless tale of sorrow
Is all unrolled in vain;
May comes to-morrow
And Ludlow fair again.

                              A.E. HOUSMAN

# Mortimer Forest

All afternoon the drone of a saw has fanned
with resin over this bank of vibrating pines;
with each completed sever, falling an octave –
the one, only, sound of another human
in all dead, hot, black Mortimer Forest.

I have seen the place; clearing, sawdust, tarpaulin,
pipe-dottle, that is all, never the man.

If it stops now and I go there I will find,
to mark hard work for so long, long weeping ranks,
curtailed, seasoning in glutinous tiers,
and dust, dust red wood-ants perpetually sift.

PETER READING


# Goodbye to the Hills

Again I watch them slope away –
– The hills I love, as eastward I
Am carried. As the train slips by
The Wrekin's lion curve I know
That though once more forsaken, they
Live in my heart as now they lie,
Leaning to Wales in one long fortress sweep,
Indigo ramparts on the rain-filled sky.

Goodbye – and yet you hold me fast, you hills.
Breidden's far peak and Caradoc's rough crest,
Desolate Long Mynd, massive shouldered Clee,
Your beauty as you flow into the west,
Lovely and changeless hills, shall go with me.

SYBIL POWIS

51

# HEREFORDSHIRE

*Hills, vales, woods, netted in a silver mist,*
*Farms, granges, doubled-up among the hills;*
*And cattle grazing in the watered vales,*
*And cottage chimneys smoking from the woods,*
*And cottage gardens smelling everywhere,*
*Confused with smell of orchards.*

ELIZABETH BARRETT BROWNING
from *Aurora Leigh*

# Border Country

The wind blows from the mountains over meadows
Whose faces have uneven shadows,
And round the sky's arena in their courses
Stumble black clouds like circus horses,
And stretching far are cornfields fat with grain
With hedges holding out dry tongues for rain,
White cottages whose twirling smoke
Now merges with dusk's darkening cloak,
And villages from Hereford to Wales
Are loud with waking nightingales.
Quick as an eel the starcaught river turns
And twists among the beds of dimming ferns,
The snail adventures in the tormentil
And rain drives down on field and hill.

LEONARD CLARK

# Note on History

Countless the larks, hysterically singing
In this wind-worried place of heather and grass
Where the ancients buried one of their number,
A chieftain, a warrior, a tamer of men.
Folklore would have us believe it was Arthur*
But names become garbled when mumbled through beards.
He rated a mound; that surely meant something,
A communal effort to honour the dead.
Perhaps in their way they tried to make certain
His ghost would not walk and trouble their dreams,
Making provision against resurrection.
Whatever the reason their secret is safe.

He lay here for centuries, lost and forgotten,
The mound and its message in this lonely place,
Till people came out to dig up its history
Then carefully carried his relics away
To store them till doomsday on museum shelving,
His name quite unknown and his deeds still unsaid.

Only the larks remember his passing,
Only the larks can sing of his fame.

EDWARD KAULFUSS

* Arthur's Stone, Dorstone Hill, Golden Valley, Herefordshire

# The Bee-Flight

(at Bredwardine)

That was a strange, rare place, in a loop
between river and nippled hill
with a crooked sandstone church and trees
that corkscrewed, and a massive leaning yew
one thousand years thick, peeled rosy flesh
and a woman carved into the north wall
with legs agape, and a man with a bird's head
whistling sorcery. The ground rose
in hummocks: the past, carelessly buried,
trying to break through. Snowdrops showed white
and wet below the mound. I stood at the cusp
of spring in a flayed landscape
bleached-out by frost, stripped clean

as an old bone, sucked dry. I'd thought
there was nothing to fill me, nothing to speak to me;
but here was rain smelling of turned earth,
the sun in watercolour, curved paths,
storybook trees, bark swirled, bulged-out and fissured
peopling the place. At the edge of a pool
a straddled oak with a hole
at eye level, forced me to stare. Birds calling, then
a humming past my ear, and again; brown bees
sailing in from the sedges, dipping down
into darkness, hollow mouth-oak, in and in
with grains of new gold. A ragged shower blew
up from the west. Something unfolding, stirring

under my feet. The lumpy, breast-topped crag
now spiralled in light; the birdman suddenly answered
by choruses of wings, and the opened thighs
of the sandstone witch by the presence of flying bees.

HILARY LLEWELLYN-WILLIAMS

# from *Songs of the Three Rivers*

(from *The Island*)

So, with alternate gloom and shine,
Teme falls by Llanfairwaterdine
To Knucklas village and Knighton Vale,
Where the felled woods lie silver-pale
With floss of silken willow-weed;
And on her face the windblown seed
Lighteth softer than thistledown
To drift and skim, like mayflies blown
To their death in June – till a tiny waft
Of light air lifteth it aloft,
And the seed goes sailing on its way,
While sweet Teme floweth without stay
Between the wild flags' clustered swords,
Where gentle, wide-horned Herefords
Bend their white-muzzled heads to drink
From muddy pools on the trampled brink;
Or stand knee-deep in the cool stream
In an unimaginable dream
And slowly swing their tails, while flies
Settle on their uncurious eyes;
Till the roofs of a rising village strown
On a steep hillside, and a tower of stone,
Stand in her path and halt her flow,
And clear Teme feels the undertow
Of denser waters that have run
From the marly dales of Corve and Clun,
And the streams of the confluent rivers mingle
In a deep pool that laps the shingle
Where the twin sisters meet and twine
Under the bridge at Leintwardine
And the two waters flow as one . . .

FRANCIS BRETT YOUNG

# On Croft Ambury

I climbed the hill where many years ago,
   The Ancient Briton made his final stand,
And gazing at the wondrous scene below,
   Thanked Him who made this lovely, peaceful land.
For far as eye could travel, were the hills,
   The streams, the woods, the rich red soil,
The verdant fields, the babbling hurrying rills,
   The age-long fight of Nature 'gainst man's toil.

Far to the west, the broken line of Wales,
   Was marked by Hergest, Hanter and the Gore;
Like galleons rigged with square top-gallant sails,
   To garner fickle winds that blow off shore;
And nearer was the long Silurian ridge,
   That runs past lovely Ludlow to the Clees,
With Wopley, Shobdon, Bircher, Wenlock Edge,
   Gatley and high Vinnals with its trees.

And to the East, as if they stand on guard,
   The Malverns rising from the Severn's plain;
And Hegdon Hill that lies beyond Bromyard,
   And in the valley Lemster's Norman fane;
And softly, grey against the dark green trees,
   Of Eaton Hill, and Dinmore's wooded slope,
The smoke that wafted slowly in the breeze,
   Marked Lemster's Town, Stoke Prior and Hope.

And further to the South I could discern,
   Beyond the glorious valley of the Wye,
Lone Garway's coloured coat of gorse and fern,
   And May Hill's clump of firs against the sky:
And Skirrid's Holy Mountain, with the rift
   That gives distinction to that pointed height,
And nestling at the foot of Ladylift,
   Old Weobley's patch of chequered black and white.

And then I saw the grandest of them all,
    A massive line of blue, and black, and grey,
Black Mountains, running like a wall
    From Pandy and Pontrilas up to Hay:
Where once King Arthur and his valiant knights,
    On evenings when the mountain air was still,
Pursued the wild red deer upon these heights,
    Or sat at leisured ease on Merbach Hill.

Then far beyond the border town of Hay,
    Naked and gaunt, without a single tree,
The Brecknock Beacons seemed to bar the way
    To Pembroke, and the stormy Irish Sea.
And as I gazed, I slipped into the past,
    And thought I saw a little cavalcade
Of men in armour, riding very fast;
    Wild Welshmen on a border raid.

And now the magic circle was complete,
    Except for hills that flanked the silvery Wye;
The Eppynts with their little fields so neat,
    Like coloured patchwork quilts, hung out to dry.
And there, within this ring of noble heights,
    The varied hues of nature in accord,
With boundless sky, and ever-changing lights,
    The pleasant fertile land of Hereford.

                                        GEOFFREY BRIGHT

## The Wye at Hereford

No common waters, by these ancient walls,
Flow from Plynlimon's distant storm-filled springs,
By many a changing mile the current brings
By Ithon's vale and Ebbw's rock-bound falls
And mountain moorlands where the curlew calls
A spell distilled of old and lovely things;
Cloud-wrapped memorials of long-dead Kings,
Forsaken castles and deserted halls.

The scattered dust of centuries lies blown
Along the valleys where the oaks are green,
Dressed by the summers of a thousand years
And all the sun and rain the years have known,
For all that is is born of what has been;
From age to age its laughter and its tears.

ROBERT WADE

The Wye at Hereford

# Bullingham, Hereford

Out from the city through a thin
half-country suburb stretched beside the river,
past a growth of whitish houses
and their brash pub, I came
to a fragment of old village,
warm red in the white of blossom –
empty red-brick house and silent stable-yard:
just as silent, though still alive,
a red-brick-Gothic monastery:
and over a little bridge, a convent,
by whose shut door the painted Christ,
baring his red heart, was anthemed
by high white notes of cider-apple trees,
line after line, in fullest bloom.

My mind, obsessed, tried vainly to superimpose
the May Fair's darker stridencies of sight and sound
on the serene pattern of this enclave.
On the still wall of the shut convent fell
the whirling shadow of the wheel, its voluntary victims
skewered to wire walls by the thrust of speed.
'Christ!' they screamed; the cry
was absorbed into warm silence,
became the silence; the shadow
faded into the flickering of leaves.
The sad banalities of a megaphoned lovesong
thinned and thinned over the river-meadows
till a few last notes died
in the triumphant whiteness of the silent anthem.
From far-away streets of the Fair
came at last only a distant pulsing,
like the beat of a red heart.

RUTH BIDGOOD

# Sheila na Gig at Kilpeck

Pain's a cup of honey in the pelvis.
She burns in the long, hot afternoon, stone
among the monstrous nursery faces
circling Kilpeck church. Those things we notice
as we labour distantly revolve
outside her perpetual calendar.
Men in the fields. Loads following the lanes,
strands of yellow hair caught in the hedges.

The afternoon turns round us.
The beat of the heart a great tongue in its bell,
a swell between bone cliffs; restlessness
that sets me walking; that second sight
of shadows crossing cornfields. We share
premonitions, are governed by moons
and novenas, sisters cooling our wrists
in the stump of a Celtic water stoop.

Not lust but long labouring
absorbs her, mother of the ripening
barley that swells and frets at its walls.
Somewhere far away the Severn presses,
alert at flood-tide. And everywhere rhythms
are turning their little gold cogs, caught
in her waterfalling energy.

GILLIAN CLARKE

# A Short Guide to the Carvings at Kilpeck

Light splays and has moulded monsters
issuing as zodiac from local sources,
still site of the world and guide to the end.
Spaces find beaks to bite into origin,
eat heads or sink tails in the dragon.
Fishes angle for men, warning birds
of the evil: a short nondescript monkey
known by hewn trees: has built a single arch
of his days. Angel tongue struck his ribs,
stopped fun embracing knowledge
so he bearded, capped his female with God.
This is human, not pig bear or bull's,
impost and vice on creation
till the mouth 'of remarkable size'
frees the waters: a slight journey into Eden,
where the phoenix orders prayer for
anathema, dancing and holy wedding.
Flames worship the tree, knot
snakes into faces, faces into snakes;
one falling, four return. Scourges
are forbidden. Praise stones,
jam hoods on cross saints.
Keep the castle peace.

ALAN HALSEY

Kilpeck Castle

# Buzzard Soaring

So long grounded

in himself, under such
feather weight

he seems to rise
out of a sack.

A dead poundage
re-assembles on the wings

spread into a sycamore key
turning. Earth breathes him out,

exhales him from his vantage,
to glide with the traffic between worlds,

the exploding galaxies of spores,
the seeds suspended in their shrouds.

The equality, the lightness here . . .
He feels his shadow separate

and travel the air, another
wanderer, another dust.

Below, history fires its
intricate acreage. Demesnes melt.

Towns bleed across ploughland.
Motorways grub like glaciers.

He suns. He sleepwalks on the wing
through this world and the next,

hearing the hormones hiss, hearing
the froth in his cells: *Re-enter*

*the inferno. Rise again as ash.*

ROGER GARFITT

# Old Song

(Written at St Weonard's, Herefordshire May 1983
remembering an afternoon above Capel-y-ffin, Powys
in summer of 1976.)


Birdsong outside my window
recalls tremblings of water.

I lay alone
deep in ferns by the stream's edge;
only the bee's hum
and the labyrinthine murmurings
entered my mind.

Birdsong and water bear away grief.
I walked home through the mountain mist
calling your name.

FRANCES HOROVITZ

# from *Serenade*

lad,
there be fields uncommon lovely there,
parterres of the wild iris and snowdrops of spring,
and dales of the orient wheat and of yews in visionary eyes
verging to the west, to Wales!

o lovely river Wye –
eye-bright, eye-bright, eye-bright
valley,
I would take thee there!

one side:
Black Mountains,
including even a hill
Henry James (chuff, chuff) climbed
to pick primroses . . .

other side:
Malvern Hills,
where Sir Edward heard his 'wild Welsh tune', captured it,
put it in the *Introduction & Allegro for Strings*,
*the* string piece of the century
(at least according to Lou Harrison, me, and a bottle of bourbon) . . .

Great Malvern, Wm Langland standing there –
a vision of the ploughman, half of mankind, and half the world
below . . .

JONATHAN WILLIAMS

# from *Wonderings*

### (*Ledbury*)

... Mine, was a little town of ancient grace,
A long street widened at a market-place,
Crossed, in its length, by two transversal ways
Doubtless the course of brooks in early days.
Within the width, a market-building stood
Propped upon weathered quarres of chestnut-wood. ...

... The little town was pleasant to the sight,
Fair, with half-timbered houses, black and white,
Shops, taverns, traffic, market, in the street,
And cobbled paving, painful to the feet.
Slowly, I came to know it, but at first
Judged of it only by its best and worst. ...

... Next to these dear delights, I knew
And loved, my daily western view:
Two fields to the canal, and then
A farm, a mill, and fields agen,
A wood, with yew-trees almost black;
A bridge with railways on its back;
A line of poplar-trees, a white
Steep, hilly roadway just in sight;
A hill, of which the stories told
That it had moved in days of old,
Glid for two days, church, manor, village,
Pump, barton, tavern, crop and tillage.
Beyond this Wonder, distant, dim,
My western vision had its rim,
And yet, when western skies were clear,
The distance hard, and rain was near,
A blueness shewed against the sky,
The Welsh Black Mountains, beyond Wye ...

JOHN MASEFIELD

69

# Carpenters

(Half-timbered cottages, Much Marcle)

Unlettered carpenters,
After four hundred years
Nothing is left of them,
Even their bones are dust.

They put the axe to oak,
The saw, adze and chisel;
Unlettered carpenters,
Nothing is left of them

Whose eyes grew narrower
From saw-pit to grave-pit;
After four hundred years
Even their bones are dust.

Unlettered carpenters,
After four hundred years,
All that is left of them –
V   V   O   O   X   X

GEOFFREY MASON

(Three of the carpenters' marks, incised
on joints at the 'framynplace'
to assist re-assembly on site)

# On Eastnor Knoll

Silent are the woods, and the dim green boughs are
Hushed in the twilight: yonder, in the path through
The apple-orchard, is a tired plough-boy
Calling the cows home.

A bright white star blinks, the pale moon rounds, but
Still the red, lurid wreckage of the sunset
Smoulders in smoky fire, and burns on
The misty hill-tops.

Ghostly it grows, and darker, the burning
Fades into smoke, and now the gusty oaks are
A silent army of phantoms thronging
A land of shadows.

JOHN MASEFIELD

Cider Press

# The Town II

All the beauty of made things
is spaced here, roofed, forgotten
under this quiet home-spun sky.
The streets, the roofs, the hills here lie,
the shepherd-coloured hills where no flocks run
to the unregarded sun.

Leaves the forest has cast out
foretell reunion in the rain
that joins them to the softened stones.
My thoughts, my tread, my breath remain.
Here lifts the Earth's adventurous back
unbent beneath a pedlar's pack.

MARGIAD EVANS

# from *The Wye*

The Wye is a wanderer, winding its way
Through pastures where cowslips and buttercups play,
Where velvety cows
Contentedly browse,
Nor worry nor care
Encounter us there.
The waters are cool
In each crystal pool
Where fat lazy trout
Swim sedately about.
The pastures are green
And the hills are serene
Where the wandering Wye
Goes murmuring by.
The river for ever is flowing and flowing
And flowing melodiously by –
The meandering, wandering Wye. . . .

. . . The river at Rhayader races along
By Builth it is still but a talkative song.
Through Hay and through Hereford onward it goes,
And it grows
As it flows.
Through the town of John Kyrle
It continues to swirl,
And where Harry of Monmouth, most valiant of kings,
Heard its low liquid notes, there it still softly sings:–

The pastures are green,
And the hills are serene,
Where the wandering Wye
Goes murmuring by.
The river for ever is flowing and flowing
And flowing melodiously by –
The meandering, wandering Wye.

DONALD HUGHES

73

# WORCESTERSHIRE

*See where the landscape curtsies; where the green*
*Of field and tree intensifies, and willows dip*
*Their long green fingers in the browning flood:*
*Where salmon leap and where a lone gull skims*
*On certain wing across the troubled stream.*
*This is Severn, and near here, half fearfully,*
*Is curbed and bridged her restless majesty.*
*But come with me where change has seen no change;*
*Where unspoiled woods kneel to the water's edge;*
*Where we can trail our town-white fingers through her course*
*And see, as we a moment thwart her way,*
*The greening hollows lift to creamy foam.*
*Here, with half closed eyes, we might be centuries back.*
*These banks where kingcups grow have never changed*
*And in the sullen murmur of the stream*
*Is held the music of eternity....*

JO HUNT
from *Severn*

# Worcestershire Lanes

This country differs from dry uplands, water hereabouts
is no white rarity. The muddy ditch
the Saxons named still moves beside the road
and milking-time soon churns the yard to sludge.

Men could build where they would; farms
five fields apart and cottages in threes up tracks
now detail slope and hollow, and lanes mizmaze
the countryside, hedges a screen for lover and for fox.

Thorn, hazel, briar make them alike, easy
to lose one's way, different in small things only –
empty beehives in a gangling orchard, a church
with no apparent parish, shock-yewed and lonely.

Sometimes these lanes go by, irrelevant as thoughts,
for miles with only magpies, padlocked gate, and crop,
a philosophic pattern to the man born locally,
to others only metaphors without a map.

MOLLY HOLDEN

# Mamble

I never went to Mamble
That lies above the Teme,
So I wonder who's in Mamble,
And whether people seem
Who breed and brew along there
As lazy as the name,
And whether any song there
Sets alehouse wits aflame.

The finger-post says Mamble,
And that is all I know
Of the narrow road to Mamble,
And should I turn and go
To that place of lazy token
That lies above the Teme,
There might be a Mamble broken
That was lissom in a dream.

So leave the road to Mamble
And take another road
To as good a place as Mamble
Be it lazy as a toad;
Who travels Worcester county
Takes any place that comes
When April tosses bounty
To the cherries and the plums.

JOHN DRINKWATER

# At Witley Court

At Witley Court
all that remain
are stones and stones
under the rain

and nests for birds
ivy and moss
all gone the same

merely a name
fountains of stone
absence and loss

tatters of wall
a roof of sky
and doors of air

so pass and pass
all that proud fame
fallen to earth

the years how long
and time how short
at Witley Court.

GAEL TURNBULL

# *At Arley*

(Worcs.)

The Severn sweeping smooth and broad
A motion to the hillside gives
Till it too liquifies and lives,
For glancing from that rushing road
I see the solid hill
Flow backward for a moment and stand still.

ANDREW YOUNG

# Floods at Bewdley

At eye level it seems to race,
the flooded river, and its added width
of white reflected light affronts the eye
expecting to see the deep familiar banks,
the mud shoals, the fishermen in waders.

A far cry this, on a cold Sunday morning,
from the lazy littoral shallows where
Severn usually runs. On the current
tumble and turn the empty drums,
the wodges of grass from upstream
broken banks, the household paraphernalia
snatched in passing. Nothing contains it,
neither stone nor the sly resilience
of sand, packed on the door sills, it progresses
in steady strength, the reversed and
swirling eddies over submarine bollards only
decorative to its passage. Channels
to drain it off it overflows; it ferries sheep
from their pastures, barrels from their dark.

It alarms us now as it should, that
moving highway through meadows. Men
worshipped it once, not inexplicably.
Only the black rain's ceasing in
the black mountains will muzzle it.

MOLLY HOLDEN

# Severn

(from *Worcestershire Suite*)

There was Welsh in the English water
That flowed from distant mountains
Where high on Plynlimon springs the Hafren.
There hawk, the buzzard and the merlin,
Westward hovers Cader Idris
And the silver Dovey.
The rushing stream passes
Through peat and pool,
Waterfall and cascade,
Spouts to Llyn Crochan,
Then sliding to Blaen Hafren
Becomes the Severn.

Joined by Clywedog, where ravens peck
At carcassed sheep, and spawning salmon
Plough the shingle bed,
It passes Llanidloes turning mills
To enter gorge and wood
To wind by castle, hill, and valley,
Meander through remote pastures
Then race through towns and under bridges
To Bewdley, Stourport, Worcester,
Where blue, red and black, the barges
Used to chug to loaded quays; where salmon
Eel, and trout were trapped and netted
And coracles rode the treacherous current:
Past Callow End, past Kempsey church
That looks from its hill across the Ham
Over shoals and willows to the Old Hills
And the blue line of the Malverns.
Downstream lie Severn Stoke and Pixham Ferry,
Its rusted chains now vanished,
No longer used to haul across the hunt.

Farther down lie Upton,
Ripple with its misericords,
All the seasons, fencing, ploughing,
Sowing, reaping,
Then Tewkesbury, Gloucester,
The estuary and the Bristol Channel,
Where tidal waters ride inland
And the river widens to port and shipping.

On the Welsh side factory chimneys smoke
And a salt breeze brings the cry of gulls
That wheel above the racing current
Far from hidden mountains and dreaming pastures.

ROBIN IVY

Bewdley

# Cathedral City

Here rises like a cliff the buff cathedral.
Here at its base the yellow river frets;
And past the corrupting hulks, the rusty springs,
The half-embedded bottles, bricks and tins,
The swans still paddle their surprising whiteness.
Here crippled tudor houses, Georgian squares,
Victorian factories smelling of vinegar,
And sooty streets closing like canyons,
Make up the common and distinguished features
Of one more English city.

One king was buried here. Another came
To hear the city's music.
A third, unhappier, from these walls looked out
And saw his last supporters die in the meadows.
These honours and disasters now are over.
Yet still the city lives.
Its eyes blink red and green at all the crossings;
Through the brown streets the traffic circulates;
Systole and diastole the workers enter,
They work and pause and then depart each evening;
And from these quadrilaterals of streets
The sounds of buses, newsboys, lathes and looms
Mingle in one discordant animal cry.

O ten times centenarian city, you
Are old. Treelike you've grown and grown
Ring upon ring through conquest and revolution.
Your centre now is rotting.
Timbers once felled to make a tudor mansion
Suffer a second fall.

The ancient parishes collapse and moulder;
And, like eccentric orators no one will heed,
Your stripped and crumbling churches stand alone
In cindery squares.
Yet, dead at the centre, still you add more rings.
Slowly, and with almost audible crackle,
Towards the haystack and the pigeoned copse,
The suburbs burn outward like a prairie fire.

FREDERICK GRICE

## from *The Malverns*

Here on the cropped grass of the narrow ridge I stand,
A fathom of earth, alive in air,
Aloof as an admiral on the old rocks,
    England below me:
Eastward across the Midland plains
An express is leaving for a sailors' country;
    Westward is Wales
Where on clear evenings the retired and rich
From the french windows of their sheltered mansions
See the Sugarloaf standing, an upright sentinel
    Over Abergavenny.

W.H. AUDEN

# from *Ryton Firs*

... 'I had a song, too, on my road,
But mine was in my eyes;
For Malvern Hills were with me all the way,
Singing loveliest visible melodies
Blue as a south-sea bay;
And ruddy as wine of France
Breadths of new-turn'd ploughland under them glowed.
'Twas my heart then must dance
To dwell in my delight;
No need to sing when all in song my sight
Moved over hills so musically made
And with such colour played. –
And only yesterday it was I saw
Veil'd in streamers of grey wavering smoke
My shapely Malvern Hills. . . .

LASCELLES ABERCROMBIE

# Worcestershire Lad

There's Hunnington and Hagley:
There's Chaddesley and Crowle,
And Yieldingtree enchanted
On Worcester's magic roll.

From Menith Wood to Mamble;
From Tardebigge to Teme,
The plum and pear in blossom
Are sweet as any dream.

By Dayhouse Bank and Dordale;
By Clent and Cutnall Green;
Through Himbleton and Hanbury
There's beauty to be seen.

With Shelsey Walsh and Shrawley;
With Stakenbridge and Stone;
With Abberley and Arley,
So much in love I've grown.

Who walks the road to Romsley,
From Wychenford or Wyre,
Will see the matchless beauty
Of England's midmost shire.

I've loved it all my life, lad,
And when it's time to die;
See I go to Kenelmstowe:
It's there that I would lie.

JO HUNT

# Pershore

The grey-green Avon nurses, cherishes the town,
Caressing the ancient bridge,
Russet and mellow as the pears
Which gave Pershore its name.
Veiled memories of Cavaliers clashing with Cromwell's men
Linger among the dreaming willows.
The hill of Bredon broods, a friendly presence,
Emanating domesticity from its green pastures and golden villages.
Bridge Street begins abruptly by the aged mill.
Tall houses, their glowing red brick faces
Of Georgian symmetry, outlined in white,
Eye each other, with dignity and elegance.
Broad Street recalls gay horse fairs, market stalls,
Of centuries gone by. The bustling atmosphere
Of commerce, now less strident, still remains,
Reminding the visitor of post houses, post horns,
And long departed coaches on their way to London.
Iron balconies, plane trees, yield a continental air
To the fleeting stranger.
Dominating all, the Abbey's majestic tower
Presides in a timeless zone of green peace,
Implanted by the monastery of old:
Symbol of serenity, inspiring music and the arts
In this, our present age.
SPRING: the frothing sea of white blossom,
Plum and damson, laps the town; creamy may
Adorns the hedges, whilst the cuckoo sings.
SUMMER'S sweet smell of plums pervades the gardens;
The lulling drone of distant harvesters is heard.
AUTUMN'S bonfires fade into WINTER'S chill,
And there is snow on Bredon Hill.

MARGARET BRAMFORD

# from *Testament*

... Quick, quick ... while there is time. ...
O best of friends, I leave you one sublime
Summer, one fadeless summer. 'Twas begun
Ere Cotswold hawthorn tarnished in the sun,
When hedges were fledged with green, and early swallows
Swift-darting, on curved wings, pillaged the fallows;
When all our vale was dappled blossom and light,
And oh, the scent of beanfields in the night!
You shall remember that rich dust at even
Which made old Evesham like a street in heaven,
Gold-paved, and washed within a wave of golden
Air all her dreamy towers and gables olden.
You shall remember
How arms sun-blistered, hot palms crack'd with rowing,
Clove the cool water of Avon, sweetly flowing;
And how our bodies, beautifully white,
Stretch'd to a long stroke lengthened in green light,
And we, emerging, laughed in childish wise,
And pressed the kissing water from our eyes.
Ah, was our laughter childish, or were we wise?
And then, crown of the day, a tired returning
With happy sunsets over Bredon burning,
With music and with moonlight, and good ale,
And no thought for the morrow. ...

FRANCIS BRETT YOUNG

# Bredon Hill

(from *A Shropshire Lad*)

In summertime on Bredon
  The bells they sound so clear;
Round both the shires they ring them
  In steeples far and near,
  A happy noise to hear.

Here of a Sunday morning
  My love and I would lie,
And see the coloured counties,
  And hear the larks so high
  About us in the sky.

The bells would ring to call her
  In valleys miles away:
'Come all to church, good people;
  Good people, come and pray.'
  But here my love would stay.

And I would turn and answer
  Among the springing thyme,
'Oh, peal upon our wedding,
  And we will hear the chime,
  And come to church in time.'

But when the snows at Christmas
  On Bredon top were strown,
My love rose up so early
  And stole out unbeknown
  And went to church alone.

They tolled the one bell only,
  Groom there was none to see,
The mourners followed after,
  And so to church went she,
  And would not wait for me.

The bells they sound on Bredon,
    And still the steeples hum.
'Come all to church, good people,'—
    Oh, noisy bells, be dumb;
    I hear you, I will come.

A.E. HOUSMAN

## *A Hill*

At dawn: first sight: black against orange,
a profile of giant rubble,
it barricades the sun.
Orange out of black,
a foliage of wrinkled copper,
light germinates in a furrow of the hill.

The phrases are apt.
The scene is not unusual.
The joy is in the attention.

The description is not a circumscribed likeness,
that is, of a delimited hill.
If never finally exact,
it is not exactly at random.

The description portrays a hill
which is discovered in the action:
an unknown hill which becomes known,
which is a likeness
and which becomes likely.

It is Bredon Hill. A name. But not merely.

Then is it a whale, dark indigo, partly submerged,
    the dorsum crusted with shellfish?
Mount Badon, with Arthur and the Table, and the
    last outpost of Empire?
Asleep, with drooping mouth, sunken eyes, an old
    man taking a nap?

Awake, a heraldic beast, its nostrils alert for the
    Malverns, staring beyond into the hills of Wales?
The Savages, their seventeenth century bones at
    Elmley Castle, under the garish monuments,
    newly repainted?

Sundial, Elmley Castle

Archaeologists from Birmingham, digging in the earth-
    works near Overbury, defining storage pits in
    the chalk?
A young couple who have modernized an old cottage at
    Great Comberton, with a Van Gogh print in the
    livingroom?
The damp, dripping through the bracken, settling
    on the backs of the sheep between the filaments
    of wool?
Or an afternoon yet to come, a picnic with sandwiches
    and cider, the children running happily on the turf,
    with bees in the gorse?

And it is not. And it is.

The description attests.
The attention becomes explicit.
The implicit becomes familiar.

It becomes an accumulation, not a hill.
But it declares a hill, a very particular hill,
a remarkable hill:
a hill which it is possible to know.

GAEL TURNBULL

# Apple Country

I am living, quite unplanned, by apple country.
Worcesters come the earliest: sea-green
with darkest red, even the flesh, veined pink.
They have a bloom no hand can brush away
sweet breath made visible. But do not think
to have them through the dark days: they'll not keep,
for that choose Coxes flecked with gold
which wrinkle into kindness, winter's fires.

Where I was born they let no flowering trees
in the bare fields, which grow my dreams, which hold
only the lasting crops: potato, wheat.
How low the houses crouch upon their soil
with fruitless hedges; at the barn's end, cars:

none yours. I have no art for probing back
to such dark roots. Yet if you pass this place
though skies shine lean with frost, no softness dapples
white wall to cave of leaf, yet stranger, knock.

For I will give you apples.

ALISON BRACKENBURY

# GLOUCESTERSHIRE

*Only the wanderer*
  *Knows England's graces,*
*Or can anew see clear*
  *Familiar faces.*

*And who loves joy as he*
  *That dwells in shadows?*
*Do not forget me quite,*
  *O Severn meadows.*

IVOR GURNEY
*Song*

# Tewkesbury

Some Dane looking out from the water-settlements,
If settlements there were, must have thought as I,
'Square stone should fill that bit of lower sky.
Were I a king and had my influence,
Farms should go up for this, flames make terror go high.
But I would set my name in high eminence.'
Forthampton walking, thinking and looking to Tewkesbury,
Where a cricketer was born and a battle raged desperate,
And mustard grew, and Stratford boys early or late
May have come, and rivers, green Avon, brown Severn, meet.
And Norman Milo set a seal on the plain –
'Here man rules; his works to be found here;
Acknowledges supremacy, his strengths to be in vain;
And gathers by a sign the broad meadows in round here.'

What is best of England, going quick from beauty,
Is manifest, the slow spirit going straight on,
The dark intention corrected by eyes that see,
The somehow getting there, the last conception
Bettered, and something of one's own spirit outshown;
Grown as oaks grow, done as hard things are done.

IVOR GURNEY

# from *Train*

### 2. *Cheltenham to Gloucester*

Crossing the Motorway
the rail runs by a bank and ditch –
Perhaps it's as cold as the coldest day.
The sky and land synchronise.

Low clouds bruise Chosen Hill,
Robin's Wood, and later Frocester.
A rug of pregnant ewes
huddles close to the fence.

Firs stand at ease
Homburged by the deepening mist.
Branches wheeze and whisper.
Poplars are an arboretum on the march.

### 3. *Gloucester to Stonehouse*

Abandoned as a far sea
heavy as the Sargasso
weeds are wedded to wet –
nobody walks here.

Where trees shadow the track
baubles of mistletoe loop down.
Boys come, armed with sticks
or long apple cutters.

Where they came for conkers
now they come to trim the parasite back.
beneath it, our lips will meet
and part. Part and meet.

The contrast of field and track
echo the green of waters
where no bridges cross,
a corniche running parallel

to unfenced prairies that stand
palm to palm
in a pretence of peace,
they never truly hold, never disengage.

TRICIA TORRINGTON

## from *The Old City – Gloucester*

Who says 'Gloucester' sees a tall
Fair fashioned shape of stone arise,
That changes with the changing skies
From joy to gloom funereal,
Then quick again to joy; and sees
Those four most ancient ways come in
To mix their folk and dust and din
With the keen scent of the sea-breeze. . . .

. . . The view from Over,
Westgate Street at night, great light, deep shadows,
The Severn meadows,
The surprising, the enormous Severn Plain
So wide, so fair
From Crickley seen or Cooper's, my dear lane
That holds all lane-delightfulnesses there
(O Maisemore's darling way!)
Framilode, Frampton, Dymock, Minsterworth . . .
You are the flowers of villages in all earth! . . .

IVOR GURNEY

# Charcoal Burners

In a dark wood that once I knew
There is a ring scored in the ground
Whose charred face stares on sullen skies
And near a well that bubbles into fern
Brown water down the muddy slopes
Twisting its snake-like threads through moss and leaves.
No singing birds now haunt this place,
Nor drifts of starred anemone,
But all the mottled eyes bulge out
From toadstools in the undergrowth.
Yet where rain falls slow through sparkless air
Trees died a thousand times in smoke and flame
And charcoal burners fed their pits of fire
With branches green as lizard skin;
Each morning saw the clearing blue with sacrifice,
Each night was red with dragons' tongues.
And once I held a chip of virgin charcoal in my hand
And wrote my shaky name upon a stone;
I felt the newness of its powdered touch,
Its blinded buds, its destined power.
And in their wattled huts the burners crouched
Sweating and grimed, like Aztec chiefs at war;
From dusk to dawn they conned the veering wind,
Drawing at upturned pipes or munching bread
As hazel, ash and alder dropped to dust.
But all is gone and every fire is dead;
This single round of turf the only epitaph.
Yet one remains to look upon the wasted scene;
His shoulders hunched with sacks, and old man stands
With silver hair half hid in leaves and mist,
And sees himself a dancing boy again
Watching the ancient miracle that turned to black
By forest alchemy the tenderest green,
And hears above the well's small chattering tongues
The voices of old fiery boughs.

LEONARD CLARK

100

The Charcoal Burners

# The Forest of Dean

Do we feel sufficiently unique,
We who live in Dean,
Or do we take for granted what we see
As if – elsewhere – this landscape could be seen,
These place names found? To me
It is a realm of childhood: hide-and-seek

Between the trees, escaping adult strife.
City centre planners get it wrong!
The world should be like this, a harmony
Of man and nature, balanced, like a song
Everyone should sing, a melody
To help us through a complicated life.

The area has character. Although
The car and television equalise
Regions, until one becomes another,
Dean remains resilient. It lies
Just beyond the norm, by being neither
Wales nor England, but a curio,

Resoundingly itself. This difference
Is vital to its charm and independence;
I would not want it otherwise. No bland
Values reign round here; there's a resplendence
Even now about it, a command
Of language and respect, a common sense

That wins one over in the subtlest ways.
The Severn is all movement to our east,
While, to our west, the Wye is in a hurry:
Between the two there's poise. It's never ceased
To captivate the traveller. Why worry?
Fetch up here. Appreciate your days.

Change abrades what once we thought secure;
One day only faded books will capture
What it is that makes this place so special.
Until then, there's mystery, there's rapture,
As when moonlight rules; when mists are spectral;
When bluebells show; when migrant birds appear. . . .

PAUL GROVES

# *The Forest*

In this lost forest sleep hovers night and day;
I sit alone and hear
Only a rustling bird or stir
Of foraging insect through the shade;
And in the beds of crinkling fern
I see the foxgloves take their turn
To bend their trumpets to the needled floor
And silently fade.
And as the points of light creep far away
Between each darkening fir,
The ghosts of all my youth appear
To knock upon my heart's locked door;
But safe in loneliness upon this solemn ground
I dare not listen to their trespassing sound,
For in the haven of this dead retreat
Where tree and light are one unfathomable green,
Past time is but a guillotine
And memory a winding-sheet.

LEONARD CLARK

# *Foresters*

Speech House, Tumps, Corse,
sheep, fern, bark, gorse.
Bream's Eaves, Scowles, Cone,
oak, ore, coal, stone.
Stroat, Naas, Brimps, Pludds,
shrimps, sprats, reens, muds.
Sling, Awre, Meend, Slade,
axe, saw, pick, spade.
Stow, Trow, Mork, Chase,
close clan, Dean race.

IVOR WATERS

# Elvers

The river gleams with fires,
bike-spokes shred the moonlight,
here at Rea where weird nets
plunge, strain, and
trickle, stout with squirming;

shoals of silver weed
in warm bore-wracked meadows
leap for their lives, and embrace
in the mesh's teasing;

their element lost
they thrash in grass,
or tumble on tide-tossed logs,
their tracks from Sargasso
petering thus
in tangling air;

soon, Aphrodite,
the word will pass among women, as
your serpents froth in pans.

DAVID ASHBEE

# The Lock-keeper

(To the Memory of Edward Thomas)

A tall lean man he was, proud of his gun,
Of his garden, and small fruit trees every one
Knowing all weather signs, the flight of birds,
Farther than I could hear the falling thirds
Of the first cuckoo. Able at digging, he
Smoked his pipe ever, furiously, contentedly.
Full of old country tales his memory was;
Yarns of both sea and land, full of wise saws
In rough fine speech; sayings his father had,
That worked a twelve-hour day when but a lad.
Handy with timber, nothing came amiss
To his quick skill; and all the mysteries
Of sail-making, net-making, boat-building were his.
That dark face lit with bright bird-eyes, his stride
Manner most friendly courteous, stubborn pride,
I shall not forget, not yet his patience
With me, unapt, though many a far league hence
I'll travel for many a year, nor ever find
A winter-night companion more to my mind,
Nor one more wise in ways of Severn river,
Though her villages I search for ever and ever.

IVOR GURNEY

106

# On Painswick Beacon

Here lie counties five in a waggon wheel.
There quick Severn like a silver eel
Wriggles through pastures green and pale stubble.
There, sending up its quiet coloured bubble
Of earth, May Hill floats on a flaming sky.
And, marvelling at all, forgetting trouble,
Here – home again – stand I!

F.W. HARVEY

# Stroudwater Shades

(Inspired by names in the Canal Record, 1890)

Once, vessels plied these muddy waters,
coal and salt and bricks their load,
'Betsy', 'Perseverance' and 'Good Intent'
from Bullo Pill to Framilode.

Then, horses trod the fronded towpath
flanked by meadows lush and bright,
and, cumbered down, the barges followed,
'Rapid', 'Endeavour', 'Guide Me Right'.

Now, weeds and rushes clog the channel,
the lonely heron fishes free
unmoved by shades of long-gone vessels,
'Valiant', 'Rocket', 'Industry'.

SHEILA SIMMONS

# On Beacon Hill

Now as we lie beneath the sky,
Prone and knotted, you and I,
Visible at last we are
To each nebula and star.

Here as we kiss, the bloodless moon
Stirs to our rustling breath; Saturn
Leans us a heavy-lidded glance
And knows us for his revenants.

Arching, our bodies gather light
From suns long lost to human sight,
Our lips contain a dust of heat
Drawn from the burnt-out infinite.

The speechless conflict of our hands
Ruffles the red Mars' desert sands
While coupled in our doubled eyes
Jupiter dishevelled lies.

Now as we loose the knots of love,
Earth at our back and sky above,
Visible at last we gather
All that is, except each other.

LAURIE LEE

# Purton Lower Bridge

Affable water lips and chats
Along iron-bound banks. A cruiser's wake
Wags unendingly after it, floats flouncing
Like cross dowagers with long memories.
Not many boats in autumn. Boys
Lend a hand with ropes, show their catch
(A dead eel). The low swung bridge
Opens when needed, smoothly, like a sliced smile.

This is the human scale: nothing too much.
But half a mile downstream sprawls Glumdalclitch,
Naked, enormous, careless, bright with mud,
Red sun squat on her, pocked by birdfeet, cables,
Monstrously tidal, impossible, uncivil,
Desirable, the lethal river Severn.

U.A. FANTHORPE

# Barges at Purton

Beyond a row of steel pontoons
where Sharpness canal reflects the sky,
the river, treacherous and mild
uncovers mud-flats soft as curd,
moulded by the ebbing tide.

In calmness, describing history,
and intimate as ancient ruins,
with picturesque tenacity
the hulks rot, stranded shoalwise,
some more grassy bank than barge
compacted in the soil which covers them.

The structure and the bulk remains,
of pitch caulked timbers
studded with iron,
stout ribs retaining graceful lines
of bow and stern,
cleats warped by hawsers
into hour-glass shapes,
tillers jammed at awkward angles
from the moment they were beached,
like remnants from outlandish fleets
left here to stem the Severn's tide.

ROGER DAVISON

Barges at Purton

# Dursley Lantern

I love to hear the wind rustle in the trees.
It is the landsman's equivalent
of listening to the Severn.

Picking sloes on Stinchcombe Hill
is like filling pebbles in a pail.
My conch is a nutshell
attuned to all those sounds
that susurrate or sough
for trees are strung like harps
by their density of leaf.

Each leaf is a shirt-tail hanging out:
A Dursley lantern
in the dialect of the wind.

MICHAEL HENRY

# Severn Bore

Somewhere out there the sea has shrugged its shoulders.
Grey-green masses slip, rise, gather
to a ripple and a wave, purposeful, arrowing up
arteries of the land. Brown and sinuous, supple
as an otter, nosing upstream under the arching
bridge, past Chepstow, Lydney, Berkeley where a king
screamed; Westbury, where the old men
click stopwatches with grins of satisfaction;
slopping into the wellingtons of watchers,
swamping the nests of coots, splashing binoculars.
And so to Minsterworth meadows where Ivor Gurney's ghost
walks in sunlight, unforgotten; past lost
lanes, cow-trodden banks, nudging the reeds,
lifting the lank waterweed,
flooding pills, backwaters, bobbing the floats
of fishermen, the undersides of leaves and boats,
and gliding, gliding, over Cotswold's flawed
reflection, the sun swelling, the blue sky scored
with ripples, fish and dragonfly, stirred
by the drip and cloop of oars; and finally, unheard,
washing into the backstreets of the town to lie
at the foot of the high
cathedral, prostrate, breathless,
pilgrim from a far place;
refugee
from the ominous petulance of the sea.

CATHERINE FISHER

# GWENT & SOUTHERN POWYS
## (Monmouthshire & Breconshire)

*The Danube to the Severn gave*
*The darken'd heart that beat no more;*
*They laid him by the pleasant shore,*
*And in the hearing of the wave.*

*There twice a day the Severn fills;*
*The salt sea-water passes by,*
*And hushes half the babbling Wye,*
*And makes a silence in the hills. . . .*

ALFRED LORD TENNYSON
from *In Memoriam A.H.H.*

# Departure in Middle Age

The hedges are dazed as cock-crow, heaps of leaves
Brushed back to them like a child's hair
After a sweat, and clouds as recently bundled
Out of the hollows whimper a little in the conifers higher up.
I am the one without tears, cold
And strange to myself as a stepfather encountered
For the first time in the passage from the front door.

But I cannot go back, plump up the pillow and shape
My sickness like courage. I have spent the night in a shiver:
Usk water passing now was a chatter under the Fan
When the first cold came on. They are all dead, all,
Or scattered, father, mother, my pinafore friends,
And the playground's echoes have not waited for my return.
Exile is the parcel I carry, and you know this,
Clouds, when you drop your pretences and the hills clear.

ROLAND MATHIAS

# In the Black Mountains

We hardly know
The consequence
Of hills. Here
On this hogback

I found an owl's
White skull, and
The delicate
Piping of bones.

It was a hill
Death, clean
Like the ruined farms
Tenanted

By grass and nettles,
And silent swathes
Of light. I stood
There a long time

The only upright
Living thing, until
A wind brought cloud
Racing its

Shadow, rushing
Up hill-slopes to
Block out the sun.
What was begun

Then is with me
Now. The hills are
Impartial, out-
Lasting the farms

And the bone eyed
Owl. An open hand
Where the truth
Lies green and still.

JOHN BARNIE

# Hang-Gliders

The boy scouts gone; the range of hills forsaken
as far as eyes can strain, and further,
apart from one man chopping bracken,
and, overhanging the burned heather,
this scarlet blot, shutting the sun out, like
some giant moth let loose on Offa's Dyke.

He rises, floats above the empty valley.
Air currents hold him, clearing swathes of mist
to show the towers of Longtown and Llanthony,
small squares of light in that immense abyss.
Cramped cells, black volumes that a lonely clerk
read all night through. Flying was devil's work.

You watch, and almost think the wind might take him
across the Severn's mouth, from Wales to Wiltshire,
to where the monk of Malmesbury lies broken,
who, in his home-made wings, climbed that tall tower,
looked out, and launched himself into the sky,
nine centuries since, to prove a man could fly.

MERRYN WILLIAMS

# The Black Mountains

The border rises
remote, temporary
as someone in thought.

A gritty suspension
of shale,
a slipknot of starlings
unties in the wind.

Where the road estuary
feeds the last farms

a man is driftwood,
hedge thin, leafless

as winds that channel
stone and hedge-fall
before Longtown

to keen
on the black slate
the headstone

Wales.
A thread of snow
along a ridge,
the gullies sewn
white.

He is out of reach
at Olchon;
a remnant of
the mountain dress

a rag piece, luck
tied to a thorn.

Touched by belief
we forbear

locked in the shadow
of our hunting dogs,
a splint of tree and bone.

Steeped
in north shadow
in outlying figures
in signs, in snow,

a trace of
something allied
domestic,
close as ourselves

remains isolate;
its distance
a wilderness in me.

TESSA LUND

# from *Green Mountain, Black Mountain*

. . . In border Powys, a landrover
stalls on a hilltrack.
A farmer gets out with a halter,
plods to a sodden field where
a mare and her colt have rolled
the wet soil of Welsh weather
all a mud-lashed winter.

Unlatching the gate, he
forces the halter on the caked
anxious head of the mare,
then leads her away to where
a plan of his own makes fast
to some spindle purpose
the fate of the three of them.

The inscrutable movements of the man
puzzle the horses, who
follow him, nevertheless,
up the piebald track,
snowdeep in drift in places,
tyre-churned with red mud.

These are the Black Mountains
where the drenched sleep of Wales
troubles King Arthur in his cave,
where invisible hankerings of the dead
trouble the farms spilled over them –
the heaped fields, graves and tales.

And he, with his brace of horses,
barker at strangers, inbreeder of races,
is Teyrnon still, or Pryderi the colt-child,
fixed without shape or time
between the ghost-pull of Annwfn –
that other world, underworld, feathering
green Wales in its word-mist –

And the animal pull of his green dunged boots,
which take him, as he takes his horses,
up a red and white track for which he has
no name. A habit. An inheritance.
A cold night's work getting lambs born.
And in the morning, again. . . .

ANNE STEVENSON


# *Well at Trellech*


this pool is full of wishes
and salmon under rushes
pass a sunken church
                    touching each wall
this pool is full of pebbles
and gently rising bubbles
is it bottomless?
                    no echoes call
this child is full of wonder
dropping dreams in water
making faint bells chime
                    he hears them all
this child has spent an hour
trying to reach the tower
once more. how far can
                    innocence fall?

ALISON BIELSKI

# Penallt, 1981

### for Tom

The rumoured snow has come good,
soft on the heels of your grief.
Like a palm over distraught fields
it is a no-nonsense nurse, in love
secretly with head-wounded hills
bandaged up to the eyes of farms.

It presses an ear close to one wall
beyond which you are back in that room,
repeating scales on a cliff-top walk,
the sharp and flat ice underfoot.

You will get it right, you will break.
Your massive heart in thaw will out
of that dark day, and death on a tightrope
will sing and cry to the quiet snow,
which smothers the mute landscape,
the lost scores of walks below.

PAUL HENRY

# from *Lines Written A Few Miles Above Tintern Abbey*

Five years have past; five summers with the length
Of five long winters! and again I hear
These waters, rolling from their mountain springs
With a soft inland murmur. – Once again
Do I behold these steep and lofty cliffs,
That on a wild secluded scene impress
Thoughts of more deep seclusion; and connect
The landscpe with the quiet of the sky.
The day is come when I again repose
Here, under this dark sycamore, and view
These plots of cottage-ground, these orchard-tufts,
Which at this season, with their unripe fruits,
Are clad in one green hue, and lose themselves
'Mid groves and copses. Once again I see
These hedge-rows, hardly hedge-rows, little lines
Of sportive wood run wild: these pastoral farms,
Green to the very door; and wreaths of smoke
Sent up; in silence, from among the trees!
With some uncertain notice, as might seem
Of vagrant dwellers in the houseless woods,
Or of some hermit's cave, where by his fire
The Hermit sits alone.

WILLIAM WORDSWORTH

Tintern Abbey

# Tintern Abbey: the white wind

(from *Guests of Silence*)

Brother, did you too know
the white wind, the sudden
violent wind which streams
downriver from the hills?

Or did you at holy office hear
a sigh, a sound of wings, a song
at one with the song of love?
Or see Christ's dear blood
stream in the stained glass
where now the wind drives through?

Would we know each other
soul to soul, you who knelt
at Calvary, world's centre
within these walls, and I
who stand in the dirt nave
open to the sky?
I do not think so – only now

I feel close to you, under
the white wind from the hills
which blasts cold and downpour
through the shell, the ruin
raised on all that is broken,
the house that is always to build.

JEREMY HOOKER

127

# Chepstow

In the grey Wye water
the silver tremor of salmon
and track of an otter.

From the moot hall ceiling
still stare the stone faces
of men whose oak ships
sailed for Gascony wine
or traded for stockfish
on the banned coast of Iceland,
when Harry of Monmouth
led his bowmen to Agincourt.

The portwall and castle
built by the Normans
to hold Gwent in awe.
Here ruled the Bigods,
the Marshals, and Clares,
Lords of the Marches,
unruly to kings.

Stones of the centuries,
streets shaped at the Conquest,
narrow disorder
winding up from the river.

IVOR WATERS

# Wild Strawberries

What I get I bring home to you:
a dark handful, sweet-edged,
dissolving in one mouthful.

I bother to bring them for you
though they're so quickly over,
pulpless, sliding to juice,

a grainy rub on the tongue
and the taste's gone. If you remember
we were in the woods at wild strawberry time

and I was making a basket of dockleaves
to hold what you'd picked,
but the cold leaves unplaited themselves

and slid apart, and again unplaited themselves
until I gave up and ate wild strawberries
out of your hands for sweetness.

I lipped at your palm –
the little salt edge there,
the tang of money you'd handled.

As we stayed in the wood, hidden,
we heard the sound system below us
calling the winners at Chepstow,
faint as the breeze turned.

The sun came out on us, the shade blotches
went hazel: we heard names
bubble like stock-doves over the woods

as jockeys in stained silks gentled
those sweat-dark, shuddering horses
down to the walk.

HELEN DUNMORE

# At Usk

On a cold day, in the churchyard, between the gate and
the west door's unlocked arch,

lay the flat stone. It was
anonymous. It might have
gained by chance its grace

of simple effigy, round
eyeless head, rough torso,
a hint of sleeping child

in its stillness; a brown
stone of Monmouthshire
shaped and polished by rain.

A child was kneeling there,
absorbed, concentrating,
measuring with happy care

on the cold of breast
and throat her offering
of snowdrop and crocus.

She matched the flowers,
placed them on the stone
child with her red fingers,

and then ran off to some
warm house in the town.
Now on the stone a film

of winter sap sticks the
limp stalks, but it is
the child at home that I

think of as I walk quickly
through God's still acre.
Her gifts delight me, and I

am leaving Usk, moving
toward the M4, clearly
right to praise the living.

LESLIE NORRIS

## *Usk*

(from Landscapes)

Do not suddenly break the branch, or
Hope to find
The white hart behind the white well.
Glance aside, not for lance, do not spell
Old enchantments. Let them sleep.
'Gently dip, but not too deep',
Lift your eyes
Where the roads dip and where the roads rise
Seek only there
Where the grey light meets the green air
The hermit's chapel, the pilgrim's prayer.

T.S. ELIOT

# Days That Have Been

Can I forget the sweet days that have been,
   When poetry first began to warm my blood;
When from the hills of Gwent I saw the earth
   Burned into two by Severn's silver flood:

When I would go alone at night to see
   The moonlight, like a big white butterfly,
Dreaming on that old castle near Caerleon,
   While at its side the Usk went softly by:

When I would stare at lovely clouds in Heaven,
   Or watch them when reported by deep streams;
When feeling pressed like thunder, but would not
   Break into that grand music of my dreams?

Can I forget the sweet days that have been,
   The villages so green I have been in;
Llantarnam, Magor, Malpas, and Llanwern,
   Liswery, old Caerleon, and Alteryn?

Can I forget the banks of Malpas Brook,
   Or Ebbw's voice in such a wild delight,
As on he dashed with pebbles in his throat,
   Gurgling towards the sea with all his might?

Ah, when I see a leafy village now,
   I sigh and ask it for Llantarnam's green;
I ask each river where is Ebbw's voice –
   In memory of the sweet days that have been.

W.H. DAVIES

# Hill Fort, Caerleon

From this tree-finned hill
Breasting the breeze –
Leaf shadows like water shifting,
Sounds of water always moving
In the preening of so many leaves –
I can look down over old Caerllion.

In the aqueous rush of bracken fronds
Breaking round, and in a sound
Clearer now, once heard,
An unbroken hum
Like some instrument endlessly strummed
On one low note, or the tone

Of wires looped from pole
To pole vibrating through wood
Where we pressed our ears,
There is a sense of something living,
Breathing, watching here
As I push towards the rampart mound.

The path is blocked. A swarthy
Sentry bars my way, his spear-
Tip sparks with sunlight.
He challenges in accents I know well;
The words I recognise, but the sense eludes.
I am ashamed and silent. He runs me through.

SAM ADAMS

# The River Severn

This is the morning bright and clear,
  To stand on top of Christchurch Hill;
We'll see the Severn, looking down,
  In all his silver beauty, Love –
Where he lies basking in the sun.

My lovely Severn shines as bright
  As any moon on trucks of coal,
Or sun above our greenest meadow;
  Till I again defy the world
To search his face and find a shadow.

W.H. DAVIES

# BRISTOL AND AVON

*City of clanging bells*
*And narrow, dingy streets,*
*Where the continuous din of traffic swells,*
*The throb of commerce beats . . .*

*. . . Close to thine ancient walls*
*Come subtle whisperings of the Severn Sea.*
*I stand upon thy quay*
*Amid the noisy calls,*
*The dissonant cries,*
*The clash and hurry of thy merchandise:*
*And with the tide that creeps*
*In stained impurity.*
*There comes a legend of far ocean deeps,*
*Of cave and crag and seaward mystery.*

ARTHUR L. SALMON
from *In the Dim City*

135

# New Passage Hotel, Pilning

Where a
quiet October sky
mirrors on low levels
of the estuary,
it stands,
where frolic windily
the yellow grasses
at seas' edges,
and, on the convex eye
shines the long bridge,
breaking the sky,
and on the soul masses
the sweep of
distances, oceans, mightily
craving notice.

RICHARD BALL

# Severn Estuary ABC

A is a hat. Sun on my head.
B binoculars I'm using
C across the water. Largest concentration.
D is design. Planned
E in Europe. Believe that.
F is mud flats, wading birds
G for godwit, green sandpiper, grey plover
H is heavy population, heavy water.
I'm informed. I watch tv. My hat is
Just there to stop the sun burning.
Know what does it?
L is little suns in bottles. Heat.
M is the mighty atom.
N for no trouble in Oldbury, Hinkley Point, Berkeley.
Old stuff, I know. They're not sure.
P soup of a public explanation.
Quantity before quality. The fuel of the future.
R is rich someone's salting somewhere. There's always someone.
Severn seeped solid. Sold down the river.
T is truth. Piece of fiction.
Ah yes.
U is understanding. It's safe.
V is very safe. Formation of ducks. Skinhead. Thatcher.
We buy it.
X marks the spot. The insidious ingress. The cancer.
Why don't we do something?
Z is the sound of us listening.

PETER FINCH

# Bristol, An Exile's View

Returning
as to some aged mother,
changed
but not destroyed
still her rich heart
fed
by river arteries,
sends
her fingers
stretching seaward,

though she's old
and multistoried scars
diminish
but can't hide
her slender elegance
and if her industries
have lined her
still her wrinkles
are endured
with dignity

but
sprightly too
confounds her critics
still expands
and throbs with life
always seeking new horizons
even in the stars
she spreads
her strong yet gentle
influence.

DAVE SAMPSON

# At Saint Mary's Church

(Bristol)

The high nave, in a place of ships,
    Seems like the invitation to some voyage
Long deferred. It will not be undertaken now.
    Saint Mary's shares a horizon
With blocks in a mock stone-brown
    Meant to resemble hers. This cheek by jowl affair
Labours to prove we can equal or outdo
    Those eras of cholera, fear of the mob.
If that is true, it is not true here.
    Elizabeth thought this church the comeliest
She had seen, and haunts it still, solid
    In painted wood, and carved by the same
Hands as those, that in a place of ships,
    Shaped gaudy figure-heads. And though
That voyage is not to be undertaken, she,
    All bright will, female insouciance,
Might well have been the thrust and prow
    To such a venture now forsaken
In the dust of abolished streets, the land-
    Locked angles of a stale geometry.

CHARLES TOMLINSON

# Bristol Re-visited

The city seems the same as my grandchild skips
Across the Clifton Downs; rain from the south-west
Mows the grass flat, it always did.
We watch the hurrying feet splash to the carparks
From Carwardine's coffee and George's bookshop.
There is blue glass against a windowpane
And a mastèd ship at the end of the street.

I remember that you said, 'I forbid you',
Yet I did come back, although I had no need to,
Unless to mourn is a necessity. Once when my shoes
Crackled the sugared glass and the rubble steamed,
Dust tasted of bitter salt on my lips;
I thought of Lot's wife looking back in tears
And climbed my way to Christmas Steps,
A place still recognisable.

There was blue glass, by a miracle, poised, intact,
It held a mastèd ship.

GUIDA SWAN

# The Cabot Memorial Tower

(As seen on approaching Bristol from Bath by train)

Lofty against the sky a tower stands,
Which boldly takes the brave salute of day,
Telling of rare adventures in strange lands,
Or looms mysterious through the twilight grey,
A pinnacled tower that bids the eyes look up
And stirs the heart and makes the pulses beat,
And beckons youth to drain the glowing cup
Of derring-do that recks not of defeat.
For this keeps green the memory of those
Whom England's Majesty from Bristol quays,
'Mid blazonings of red rose and white rose,
Bade forth to chart the yet uncharted seas,
John and Sebastian Cabot, whose renown
Crowns their dear city with deathless crown.

E.B.W. CHAPPELOW

The Cabot Tower

# Bristol Fashion

Brig-stow the bridge-place
(between ocean, space?)
spanning enigma of caution
in adventurous face;

equating Vincent, Goram,
giants hewing a gorge,
with cash on the nail, slave dealing,
evangelical zeal;

where lie in catalytic eyes
Canynges' fervour, Cabot twinkling on,
an iron glint of Brunel,
a Chattertonian tear;

where coldly blue as Bristol glass
seem the lads before light gleams through,
Where the smooth-skinned, golden lasses
are sweet-kissed as Bristol Cream;

where queenly Clifton arches her back
and stretches for a crown of Downs,
where Blackboy bows to Whiteladies
while Filton tunes the Mach X sounds.

Seasplash, skyflash
in the stolid spirit of Bristol fashion
for those who would slow
to feel a city's glow.

ROBIN LLOYD

# Eastville Park

I sat on a bench in Eastville Park
It was Monday the 28th of October
I am your old intentions she said
And all your old intentions are over.

She stood beside me, I did not see her
Her shadow fell on Eastville Park
Not precise or shapely but spreading outwards
On the tatty grass of Eastville Park.

A swan might buckle its yellow beak
With the black of its eye and the black of its mouth
In a shepherd's crook, or the elms impend
Nothing of this could be said aloud.

I did not then sit on a bench
I was a shadow under a tree
I was a leaf the wind carried
Around the edge of the football game.

No need for any return for I find
Myself where I left myself – in the lurch
There are no trams but I remember them
Wherever I went I came here first.

C.H. SISSON

# Stones of Bristol

They write of the Cathedral, whose old walls,
Brought here from Dundry quarries, make their stand,
Grave and benign, and of the Lord Mayor's Chapel tower
Lifting pink sandstone to the sky, and cite
The carvings on St. Mary's church, always
In flower, but I would also celebrate
Those randomly split shapes of local rock
Patiently pieced in walls, after
The craftsman's own free judgment, and his way
With all their colours: cinnamon and peach,
Carnation, crimson, white of hellebore . . .
One garden wall is like a bastion
Of roses . . . Men who plotted these mosaics
Carried hand-hods for mortar perched upon
Their wrists like birds, even sometimes called hawks,
And it is said this was the tool that Hamlet meant.
I doubt the Prince of Denmark knew the mason's craft –
Nor did my West County forbears, and yet
I find them in this stone vernacular:
The way they lived and thought; I almost see
The Bristol grandmother I never knew.

FREDA BROMHEAD

# Bristol

Green upon the flooded Avon shone the after-storm-wet-sky
Quick the struggling withy branches let the leaves of autumn fly
And a star shone over Bristol, wonderfully far and high.

Ringers in an oil-lit belfry – Bitton? Kelston? who shall say? –
Smoothly practising a plain course, caverned out the dying day
As their melancholy music flooded up and ebbed away.

Then all Somerset was round me and I saw the clippers ride,
High above the moonlit houses, triple-masted on the tide,
By the tall embattled church-towers of the Bristol waterside.

And an undersong to branches dripping into pools and wells
Out of multitudes of elm trees over leagues of hills and dells
Was the mathematic pattern of a plain course on the bells.*

|    |   |   |   |   |   |   |   |   |   |   |
|----|---|---|---|---|---|---|---|---|---|---|
| *1 | 2 | 2 | 4 | 4 | 5 | 5 | 3 | 3 | 1 | 1 |
| 2  | 1 | 4 | 2 | 5 | 4 | 3 | 5 | 1 | 3 | 2 |
| 3  | 4 | 1 | 5 | 2 | 3 | 4 | 1 | 5 | 2 | 3 |
| 4  | 3 | 5 | 1 | 3 | 2 | 1 | 4 | 2 | 5 | 4 |
| 5  | 5 | 3 | 3 | 1 | 1 | 2 | 2 | 4 | 4 | 5 |

JOHN BETJEMAN

# Clifton Suspension Bridge

Across the Gorge the man-made dream
is etched against the sky;
the cry of sea birds, far below,
is mingled with the slow,
insistent murmur of the rising tide.
A single ship slips by,
a silent toy returning home
that leaves a fringe of lace-edged foam
to lap the dark brown Avonside.

Brunel – no less than Plimsoll on the quay –
can rest content
to know how well their work was done.
The sun makes evening shadows
on the passing cars across the bridge
with tartan patterns
through the latticed steel;
you feel the trees across the way
will stay as sentinels
on guard throughout the night.

The autumn glory of the leaves
is burnished copper in the dying light,
until,
when time of celebration shall commend,
the moon pays homage
to the pendant lights that hang
a brilliant necklace, looping high,
across the Clifton sky . . .

JOHN TOMPKINS

# Camera Obscura

We scry,
using the rough white bowl –
in the dark,
passing the handle
one to other.

Men
walk upside down
in water-colour
colours.
The sky

swings through a circle.
I con
the earth
with a
concave eye.

In this dark room
high
in a light-drowned tower,
we lean
on the oar

to steer
the oyster world.
Over the mirror
of mothering shell
both birds and bridges fly.

ANNEMARIE AUSTIN

# Stanton Drew

First you dismantle the landscape.
Take away everything you first
Thought of. Trees must go,
Roads, of course, the church,
Houses, hedges, livestock, a wire
Fence. The river can stay,
But loses its stubby fringe
Of willows. What do you
See now? Grass, the circling
Mendip rim, with its notches
Fresh, like carving. A sky
Like ours, but empty along
Its lower levels. And earth
Stripped of its future, tilted
Into meaning by these stones,
Pitted and unemphatic. Re-create them.
They are the most permanent
Presences here, but cattle, weather,
Archaeologists have rubbed against them.
Still in season they will
Hold the winter sun poised
Over Maes Knoll's white cheek,
Chain the moon's footsteps to
The pattern of their dance.
Stand inside the circle. Put
Your hand on stone. Listen
To the past's long pulse.

U.A. FANTHORPE

# Clevedon

(To Ruby Finch)

When you have wakened from your deep, deep sleep,
Recreated, rested, and restored, to keep
The tryst with that great company of light,
And walk with them elysian fields all white
With stars – suddenly a dear remembrance,
Like a sweet zephyr blown by happy chance,
May come to you in that high state of bliss;
And you will pause, and turn to think of this,
And bending earthward look with loving eyes
And see these far off hills 'neath quiet skies;
And come perchance with swift untiring feet,
To where the Severn and the Avon meet;
And take again the old path by the shore,
By the Green Beach, where seagulls dip and soar,
Over unresting tides, with flashing wing,
Above the cliffs' edge, where the wild bird sing
In tangled thickets – where the tall elms range
With varied beauty as the seasons change,
Where in the folded hills the old Church keeps
Its guard above the grave where Hallam sleeps.

      *     *     *     *

An added peace shall fall upon the place,
A benediction as a Sabbath grace,
A radiance, and a singing in the air,
And I shall surely know that you are there.

REX F. HOPES

# Brean Down

There where the last grey hills come down,
Down to the sea from Mendips' crown,
And, struggling yet, the land meets sea,
Where wild thyme grows, and birds are free,
And winds blow full from the open west,
Fresh ever on their world-wide quest,
There, with the sea around me, I
Joyfully watched the sea-birds fly,
Hover and fall, their spread wings curled;
And marvelled how like smoke they whirled
About the cliffs and took no hurt.
I lay, crushing the thyme. My shirt
Blew open at the throat, wind-stirred.
Above in jewelled notes I heard
Lark with lark striving, emulous.
I saw the water tremulous
With golden laughter on its lips,
And smoke-wreaths where the stately ships
Were straining up to open sea, –
Straining, straining exultantly . . .

ERIC WALTER WHITE

# from *The Bristol Channel*

So far away she felt his first embrace,
And as their courtship slow
Moved on its ebb and flow
She yet saw nothing of his aged face.
Her beauty blossomed on his swelling tide
To where the Severn grown into the sea,
Kissed by the sun, and decked like any bride,
Moaned in tidal ecstasy.
In white array the virgin stream was wed,
And sun had scarcely set
Before two lovers met,
And Neptune took Sabrina to his bed.

BRIAN WATERS

# Fathom Five

The stream has found its mouth
and tide of satisfaction;
Here its waters stay
In calm-anointed strength
Alone and isolated.
We sail on into wide white seas
For further visitations,
Born strange and high
On waves of bewilderment
Out and beyond the range
Of former voices
Into the seas wide and white with new meaning.
Out and beyond the beam
Winking faintly over the harbour
The grief of drowned seamen
Who in coral and bone
Remember no charts
Nor the day of their foundering.

LEONARD CLARK

St Tekla's Island

# INDEX OF FIRST LINES

First you dismantle the landscape.                                    150
Five years have past; five summers with the length                    125
From high Plynlimon's shaggy side                                      11
From this tree-finned hill                                            133

Gaunt bulwark, grown out of rock and stone,                           20
Great sandstone rock, steep fashioned for defence                     49
Green upon the flooded Avon shone the after-storm-wet-sky            147

Here lie counties five in a waggon wheel.                            107
Here on the cropped grass of the narrow ridge I stand,               85
Here rises like a cliff the buff cathedral.                          84
High on the hill the curlews and the whimbrels,                      34
High the vanes of Shrewsbury gleam                                   41
Hills, vales, woods, netted in a silver mist,                        53

I am living, quite unplanned by apple country.                      94
I climbed the hill where many years ago,                            59
I drive with the sun at my back                                     44
... 'I had a song, too, on my road,                                 86
I love to hear the wind rustle in the trees.                        112
I never went to Mamble                                               78
I sat on a bench in Eastville Park                                  145
I, who go back to my world,                                         37
In a dark wood that once I knew                                     100
... In border Powys, a landrover                                    122
In summertime on Bredon                                             90
In the grey Wye water                                               128
In this lost forest sleep hovers night and day;                    103
It fell upon an April day,                                          27

lad, there be fields uncommon lovely there,                        68
Light splays and has moulded monsters                              64
Lofty against the sky a tower stands,                              142
Long since, when coming from the West,                             43

... Mine, was a little town of ancient grace,                      69
Montgomery's hills are deeply brown,                               18

No common waters, by these ancient walls,                          60
Now as we lie beneath the sky,      ·                              108

# INDEX OF POETS

161

# Information on Albums and Settings

The following poems from this anthology have been set to music by Johnny Coppin:

'On Beacon Hill' by Laurie Lee – recorded on the *Edge of Day* album 1989. Red Sky Records.

'On a Hill in Shropshire' by Margery Lea – recorded on the *Force of the River* album 1993. Red Sky Records and featured in the Shrewsbury Theatre Guild's production of *Arthur's Plough* by Arthur Hollins, adapted by Chris Eldon Lee, 1991.

'The Shropshire Friends' by John Masefield – broadcast on BBC Radio Shropshire 1988.

Extracts from 'Who Killed Prees Heath?' by Eleanor Cooke – composed for the Shrewsbury Theatre Guild production 1992.

'Worcestershire Lad' by Jo Hunt – composed for Countess of Huntingdon Hall, Worcester concert 1993.

### Discography

*Roll on Dreamer* 1978. Reissued 1992. Red Sky RSKC 102
*No Going Back* 1979. Rola R 002
*Get Lucky* 1982. Starward SWL 2003
*Forest and Vale and High Blue Hill* 1983. Red Sky RSKC 015
　　Poems of Gloucestershire with settings of Ivor Gurney, Leonard Clark, Laurie Lee, F.W. Harvey, John Drinkwater, Frank Mansell, Eva Dobell and John Haines.
*Line of Blue* 1985. Red Sky RSK 106/RSKC 106
*English Morning* 1987. Red Sky RSK 107/RSKC 107
　　Songs of Gloucestershire and beyond, with settings of Ivor Gurney, John Masefield, Leonard Clark, W.H. Davies, Frank Mansell, John Drinkwater, Edward Shanks, Eva Dobell, and Edward Berryman.

*Edge of Day* (with Laurie Lee) 1989. Red Sky RSK 108/RSKC 108/ RSKCD 108

A seasonal anthology in words and music – a tribute to the poetry of Laurie Lee.

*The Glorious Glosters* (with Band of Glos. Regt) 1990. Red Sky RSK 109/RSKC 109

Includes settings of Gurney, Harvey, Clark, and Mansell.

*Songs on Lonely Roads – The Story of Ivor Gurney* (with David Goodland) 1990. Red Sky RSKC 110

A 90-min. musical drama telling the story of one of Britain's finest composers and war poets through his letters and poems.

*West Country Christmas* 1990. Red Sky RSKC 111/RSKCD 111

Includes settings of Charles Causley, Thomas Hardy, and Leonard Clark.

*Force of the River* 1993. Red Sky RSKC 112/RSKCD 112

Songs written in the border counties and includes a setting of Margery Lea's 'On a Hill in Shropshire'.

All albums on Red Sky Records are available at good record shops (via Topic, CM, and ADA Distributors) and by Mail Order direct from Red Sky Records. For a catalogue and price list please write to: Red Sky Records, P.O. BOX 7, Stonehouse, Glos. GL10 3PQ, UK.

If you would like to join the mailing list for news of future concerts, album releases, and books, then please send your name and address to Red Sky Records.